D0203737

# Serious Daring from Within

**Recent Titles in**
**Contributions in Women's Studies**

The President's Partner: The First Lady in the Twentieth Century
*Myra G. Gutin*

Women War Correspondents of World War II
*Lilya Wagner*

Feminism and Black Activism in Contemporary America: An Ideological Assessment
*Irvin D. Solomon*

Scandinavian Women Writers: An Anthology from the 1880s to the 1980s
*Ingrid Claréus, editor*

To Bind Up the Wounds: Catholic Sister Nurses in the U.S. Civil War
*Sister Mary Denis Maher*

Women's Life Cycle and Economic Insecurity: Problems and Proposals
*Martha N. Ozawa, editor*

The Question of How: Women Writers and New Portuguese Literature
*Darlene J. Sadlier*

Mother Puzzles: Daughters and Mothers in Contemporary American Literature
*Mickey Pearlman, editor*

Education for Equality: Women's Rights Periodicals and Women's Higher Education, 1849–1920
*Patricia Smith Butcher*

Women Changing Work
*Patricia W. Lunneborg*

From the Hearth to the Open Road: A Feminist Study of Aging in Contemporary Literature
*Barbara Frey Waxman*

Women, Equality, and the French Revolution
*Candice E. Proctor*

# SERIOUS DARING FROM WITHIN

## Female Narrative Strategies in Eudora Welty's Novels

FRANZISKA GYGAX

*Contributions in Women's Studies, Number 114*

GREENWOOD PRESS

New York · Westport, Connecticut · London

**Library of Congress Cataloging-in-Publication Data**

Gygax, Franziska.
Serious daring from within : female narrative strategies in Eudora Welty's novels / Franziska Gygax.
p. cm.—(Contributions in women's studies, ISSN 0147-104X ; no. 114)
Includes bibliographical references (p. ).
ISBN 0-313-26865-7 (lib. bdg. : alk. paper)
1. Welty, Eudora, 1909– —Criticism and interpretation.
2. Welty, Eudora, 1909– —Characters—Women. 3. Women in literature. 4. Narration (Rhetoric) I. Title. II. Series.
PS3545.E6Z69 1990
813'.52—dc20 90-2732

British Library Cataloguing in Publication Data is available.



Library of Congress Catalog Card Number: 90-2732
ISBN: 0-313-26865-7
ISSN: 0147-104X

First published in 1990

Greenwood Press, 88 Post Road West, Westport, CT 06881
An imprint of Greenwood Publishing Group, Inc.

Printed in the United States of America

The paper used in this book complies with the Permanent Paper Standard issued by the National Information Standards Organization (Z39.48-1984).

10 9 8 7 6 5 4 3 2 1

**Copyright Acknowledgments**

The author and publisher gratefully acknowledge the following sources for granting permission to reprint:

Excerpts from *Delta Wedding* and *The Golden Apples* by Eudora Welty are reprinted by permission of Russell & Volkening as agents for the author. Copyright © 1945, renewed in 1973 by Eudora Welty; 1947, renewed in 1975 by Eudora Welty.

Excerpts from *The Golden Apples,* copyright 1947 and renewed 1975 by Eudora Welty, reprinted by permission of Harcourt Brace Jovanovich, Inc.

Excerpts from *Delta Wedding,* copyright 1946 and renewed 1974 by Eudora Welty, reprinted by permission of Harcourt Brace Jovanovich, Inc.

Excerpts from *Losing Battles* and *The Optimist's Daughter* by Eudora Welty are used with the permission of Random House, Inc. *Losing Battles* copyright © 1970 by Eudora Welty; *The Optimist's Daughter* copyright © 1969, 1972 by Eudora Welty.

The quotation from "The Song of Wandering Aengus" from *The Collected Poems of W. B. Yeats* (1961) by Yeats, used with the permission of Macmillan Publishers, Ltd.

The poem No. 309 by Emily Dickinson is reprinted from *Emily Dickinson Face to Face* by Martha D. Bianchi. Copyright 1932 by Martha Dickinson Bianchi. Copyright © renewed 1960 by Alfred Leete Hampson. Reprinted by permission of Houghton Mifflin Co.

*For largest Woman's Heart I knew—*
*'Tis little I can do—*
*And yet the largest Woman's Heart*
*Could hold an Arrow—too—*
*And so, instructed by my own,*
*I tenderer, turn Me to.*

—Emily Dickinson, No. 309

# Contents

# Acknowledgments

I wish to thank those who have helped me in writing this book in various ways. Most of all, I wish to express my deep gratitude to Eudora Welty, who received me generously in her home in Jackson, Mississippi, in 1983. Meeting her has been an experience in my life with the "Weltian order" that I would never have wanted to miss.

I thank Professor Fritz Gysin of the English Department, Berne University, for his advice and criticism; Anne Zimmermann, my former colleague from Berne, for her encouragement, faith, and the various invaluable suggestions; and Elizabeth Kaspar-Aldrich and Thomas Pughe for their meticulous readings. I am grateful also to the Swiss National Foundation for the Sciences and Humanities, whose grant enabled me to spend a year in the United States, where I had the opportunity to meet and make friends at the English Departments of the University of Massachusetts at Amherst and the University of North Carolina at Chapel

Hill. In Chapel Hill, Melanie Sabety Topp, as friend, housemate, and critical reader, deepened my knowledge and understanding of southern culture. Louis D. Rubin, Jr., kindly helped me get in touch with Eudora Welty. I thank Michael Mueller for his patience, support, and willingness to give me time off from our mutual child-care duties.

# Abbreviations of Welty's Works

| | |
|---|---|
| *DW* | *Delta Wedding*. New York: Harcourt, Brace, 1946. |
| *ES* | *The Eye of the Story: Selected Essays and Reviews*. New York: Random House, 1978. |
| *GA* | *The Golden Apples*. New York: Harcourt, Brace, 1949. |
| *LB* | *Losing Battles*. New York: Random House, 1970. |
| *OWB* | *One Writer's Beginnings*. Cambridge, Mass.: Harvard University Press, 1984. |
| *OD* | *The Optimist's Daughter*. New York: Random House, 1972. |

1

# Introduction

Eudora Welty's work has only very recently been approached from a feminist perspective.[1] Most critics have dealt with Welty as particularly southern: they have analyzed her work with a focus on her southern background and her status as a southern writer.[2] Eudora Welty's own statements about the "woman question" might be another reason why (feminist) critics have rather chosen other women writers for an analysis of *écriture féminine*.[3] In several interviews Welty has made it quite clear that she does not believe in all the issues of the women's movement,[4] and that as a writer she has never suffered any discrimination because of her sex.[5] One might conclude from such observations that no distinct expression of a female literary identity can be detected in her books, or, at least, that no such identity is consciously presented. Moreover, in Welty's fiction explicit female rebellion against patriarchal society with concrete suggestions for alternative forms of life does not occur. Yet even if an author does not explicitly refer to the difficulties she may face as a woman writer—Virginia Woolf is the most famous representative to have expressed her reluctance to use man's language[6]—a feminist critic's approach to her writing, using a completely different set of questions, can lead to new and different insights. Such, indeed, is the claim expressed by Annette Kolodny.

> All the feminist is asserting, then, is her own equivalent right to liberate new (and perhaps different) significances from these same texts; and, at the same time, her right to choose which features of a text she takes as relevant because she is, after all, asking new and different questions of it.[7]

Before asking "new" and "different" questions of Welty's texts, it is necessary to discuss possible criteria of *écriture féminine*. The French feminist critics have been the first to acknowledge theoretically that language is gendered and that gender influences writing as well as reading. Thus, the specificity of woman's language has become a central issue in feminist criticism. How do women use man's language, and is woman's language different from man's language? To find tentative answers to these complex questions, we must first consider woman's place in culture and society.

Women live and take part in our culture and society, but they nevertheless belong to the "muted group."[8] Gerda Lerner comments on this duality determining women's lives:

> Women live their social existence within the general culture and, whenever they are confined by patriarchal restraint or segregation into separateness (which always has subordination as its purpose), they transform this restraint into complementarity (asserting the importance of woman's function, even its "superiority") and redefine it. Thus, women live a duality—as members of the general culture and as partakers of women's culture.[9]

The model of women's culture outlined by Shirley and Edwin Ardener also illustrates that women partake in the male, that is, the dominant, sphere, but they also belong to a sphere in which men are not represented.[10] Edwin Ardener uses two circles that almost overlap; the larger space is occupied by both men and women. The crescent-shaped space is "women's space" or women's zone of difference.[11] As Elaine Showalter points out, this model is especially applicable to feminist literary theory since it is based on the concepts of the dominant versus the muted group.[12] The space that Ardener designates as "wild" because it is "the non-social,"[13] belongs to the "silent" women. The French feminist Claudine Herrmann refers to this very space, maintaining that woman has always needed some distance between herself and man's world:

> She must conserve some space for herself, a sort of *no man's land*, which constitutes precisely what men fail to understand of her and often attribute to stupidity because she cannot express its substances in her inevitably alienated language.[14]

The woman writer, who is forced to use the dominant language, moves in a zone that Claudine Herrmann also calls the "void,"[15] Hélène Cixous the "Dark Continent," which "is neither dark nor unexplorable."[16] This (female) space in women writers' texts can thus be filled with everything that is not expressed by the discourse in the dominant language, that has been repressed or ignored. As Sandra Gilbert and Susan Gubar have pointed out, there are persistent images in women's writings, which indicates that women writers try to express their confinement and their restrictions.[17] But, as mentioned above, they cannot express their images and themes in their own language; therefore their language is a "double-voiced discourse"[18] and also reflects a "double consciousness."[19] The woman writer puts *her* viewpoint in the medium of *his* language.

The resulting tensions can take very different forms, and, indeed, texts by women writers reflect a wide range of specific appropriations of traditional language. A striking example of this use is Gertrude Stein's *Patriarchal Poetry*, which ironically questions hegemonic patriarchal poetry.[20] Not all texts by women writers so conspicuously illustrate a "female imagination"[21] by "breaking the sentence" and "breaking the sequence."[22] Especially narrative texts reveal that there are characteristics indicative of a female authorship indiscernible after a first reading because the authors always write within their cultural heritage and many of them do not intentionally break the sentence, which, as Virginia Woolf puts it, is "made by men."[23] Thus, a description of the double-voiced discourse will always be a complex and multifarious undertaking because the feminist critic must explore the "empty space" mentioned above and—almost paradoxically—look for meaning there.

Various feminist literary studies focus on thematic aspects and often describe characteristic traits of female protagonists in literary works.[24] The search for specifically female themes and images is a frequent topic. Myth criticism has also proved to be rewarding for an analysis of women's fiction.[25] More recent studies rely on structuralist and deconstructionalist methods. Especially, analyses of plot developments illustrate that women writers devise stories for their female protagonists that differ from their male counterparts.[26] In particular, plots by twentieth-century women writers no longer conform to the traditional romance plot; instead, these plots implicitly criticize our androcentric culture.[27]

This brief enumeration of different approaches illustrates that pluralism is a characteristic of feminist criticism, a fact that Elaine Showalter sees as a danger, because the feminist critic might run the risk of using "the male critical theory."[28] I suggest that this pluralism need not rely exclusively on male theorists, but should use those theories that might prove applicable to a feminist point of view. Indeed, many feminist literary studies relying on a particular theory by a male critic throw light on the specificity of female writing. Especially in the fields of psychoanalysis, myth criticism, formalism, structuralism, and deconstruction, feminist critics use these theories successfully; sometimes it is necessary to question certain starting points or revise some ideas in order to make an inclusion of a feminist perspective possible.[29]

As mentioned at the beginning, few critical studies on Eudora Welty have observed that she writes fiction that reflects a specifically female appropriation of traditional narrative structures. Although her style has been described as "entirely feminine"[30] by Louis D. Rubin, most critics do not try to find out how this feminine style works. Rubin uses the term "feminine" as a characteristic of "elusive," "fastening on little things," "rich in allusions and connotation."[31] He characterizes Welty's style as being both "feminine" *and* "muscular,"[32] implying that feminine style can include control and preciseness in narration. But Rubin does not relate his observations to the author's sex, nor does he take into account that it is exactly the duality generating from "feminine" and "muscular" that has its own dynamics. Peggy Prenshaw is one of the first critics who insisted on Welty's status as a woman writer using gender-determined language. In her essay "Woman's World, Man's Place: The Fiction of Eudora Welty,"[33] she sets out to prove that in Welty's fiction the presence of the matriarchal world dominates. She distinguishes furthermore between a "matriarchal and feminine presence" and the masculine. Her title "Woman's World, Man's Place" is chosen to illustrate that the presence of the matriarchal (biological life; relation to the mother) and the feminine (the feminine archetype of the unconscious; according to Neumann also the archetype of psychic development)[34] have more influence on Welty's characters than the masculine principle (realm of the heroic, egoistic). With regard to the matriarchal and feminine presence, Prenshaw mentions the ancient myths of Demeter and Persephone and points out how these myths can be traced in *Delta Wedding*.[35]

Julia L. Demmin and Daniel Curley also draw our attention to Welty's use of (classical) female myths. In their analysis of *The Golden Apples* they demonstrate how female power expressed by ancient female mysteries gradually replaces male power. This transition of a male-oriented society to a female magical power is reflected in the structure of the book.[36]

Both Prenshaw's and Demmin and Curley's short studies are indicative of a Weltian strategy that has yet to be explored and analyzed further.[37] In their theoretical approach, neither of the two studies assumes the observations made above concerning female writing. In contrast, two more recent studies by Patricia Yaeger on *The Golden Apples* focus on Welty's specifically female appropriation of a male tradition from an explicitly feminist literary critic's perspective.[38] Yaeger's starting point is the assumption that a woman writer uses her own ideas and meanings while still speaking in the patriarchal language. In her book on the three southern women writers Eudora Welty, Carson McCullers, and Flannery O'Connor, Louise Westling makes a further contribution to a feminist reading. She emphasizes the influence of Virginia Woolf on Welty, stating that in *Delta Wedding* she relies on themes of womanhood similar to Woolf.[39] Westling develops her arguments mainly with respect to *Delta Wedding* and *The Golden Apples*, whereas Welty's other two novels, *Losing Battles* and *The Optimist's Daughter*, are only more or less briefly mentioned.

The most recent full-length study dealing exclusively with Welty is also written by a woman critic receptive of a female writing tradition. In Carol S. Manning's book *With Ears Opening Like Morning Glories: Eudora Welty and the Love of Storytelling*, we find various references to gender restrictions regarding female characters in Welty's work. Yet, as the title of the study indicates, the main focus is on storytelling and its southern tradition.

With respect to the tradition of the woman writer in the South, Anne Goodwyn Jones's extensive and informative study gives a survey of the roots of southern women writers covering the period between 1859 and 1936. All the writers she analyzes are white and come from an upper-middle-class background.[40] Jones sets out to describe the characteristics of southern womanhood, maintaining that the combination of the race and sex problems especially contributed to the image of the white lady. Slavery reinforced the passive position the white lady occupied; the white lady sometimes saw her female identity undermined by the black mammy on the one hand, yet often felt close to her on the other.

As Jones points out, early southern women writers do not belong to the female subculture's mainstream because their works were mostly well received by their male public: the southern gentleman "learned to appreciate a beautiful poem by a beautiful woman."[41] The southern woman writer was also linked with the works produced by southern male writers of the nineteenth and early twentieth century; these works never gained the reputation of the works by their northern compatriots, and, according to Jones, the authors mainly produced flawed, popular literature. Southern literary men felt strongly that they did not belong to the famous literary movement of the North. In this respect the woman writer did not experience "the anxiety of authorship"[42] because her male colleagues were no outstanding literary authorities. Many southern women writers raised their voices against slavery and against the extremely patriarchal southern society, but they nevertheless used a strategy common among women writers: they often masked their criticism behind seemingly trivial topics.[43] Anne Goodwyn Jones's study on seven women writers concludes with Margaret Mitchell's *Gone With the Wind*, published in 1936. Scarlett O'Hara's well-known maxim, "Tomorrow is another day," implying belief in the future, is symbolically indicative of the fruitful work to be done by the southern women writers of the Southern Literary Renascence.

Eudora Welty, as an exemplary figure among these women writers, began to write in the thirties, when she returned back to Jackson, Mississippi, after spending a year studying in New York. Almost all of her work is deeply rooted in the southern world. She is called a regional writer in earlier studies because the sense of place is so conspicuous in her work, but more recent studies praise her as a writer who contributed more to American literature than only an excellent depiction of a certain region.[44] Chester Eisinger's attempt to place Welty in a tradition provides an insight into the complexity of the various strands of literary influences in her work. Eisinger calls her a "transition figure"[45] belonging both to the realistic and experimental modernist traditions. He also adheres to Welty's own ideas about fiction collected in *The Eye of the Story* and concludes that she believes in the mimetic function of fiction but at the same time insists on the writer's imagination, which is ultimately reflected in her medium:

> Subject, method, form, style, all wait upon—indeed hang upon—a sort of double thunderclap at the author's ears: the break of the living world upon what is already stirring inside the mind, and the answering impulse that in a moment of high consciousness fuses impact and image and fires them off together.[46]

Welty's contribution to modernism must be viewed with respect to women writers' share in this movement. Eisinger significantly mentions Virginia Woolf's influence on Welty.[47] It is especially the similar treatment of female characters by these women writers (e.g., Virginia Woolf, Dorothy Richardson, or Gertrude Stein) that is striking. Commenting on their contribution to modernism, Judith Kegan Gardiner points out that

> male fiction often splits characters into disjunct fragments, while female characters in novels by women tend

> to dissolve and merge into each other. The model of the integrated individual was predominantly male, and women writers show that this model of characterization is inappropriate to their experience.[48]

We will later see that many of Welty's female characters are examples of this fusion of different female characters. Yet, it is not the aim of this study to describe Welty's work in terms of the modernist movement. The observations above should only serve as an illustration of a more general aspect of Welty's share in a women writers' tradition.

As outlined above, no comprehensive feminist study has focused on all of Welty's novels so far. The title of my study, "Female Narrative Strategies in Eudora Welty's Novels," implies that my analysis of Welty's fiction will envisage issues of the recent discussions of narratology. The theory of reading and definitions of a narrative grammar provide us with models that we can use in respect to an analysis of the double-voiced discourse. If, as Jonathan Culler puts it, semiotics does not have literary works as its object, but their "intelligibility; the ways in which they make sense,"[49] an analysis of narrative strategies as used by members of the "muted group" can reveal insights into the woman writer's use of language and will finally help to elucidate the "Dark Continent."

I use the term "narrative strategies" in the first place to describe how a text refers to another or to others and how the author of a story or novel chooses from the system of language, the *langue* as it were. The expression of the choice, the *parole*, is mirrored in the text, or actually *is* the text. Furthermore, the distinction between *story* and *discourse* in a narrative is useful for us because *story*, "a sequence of actions or events, conceived as independent of their manifestation in discourse," is determined by *discourse,* "the discursive presentation or narration of events."[50] The specific appropriation of the dominant language women writers supposedly make is reflected in the discourse.

However, I shall not exclusively rely on narratological theories. At the beginning of this chapter I have mentioned pluralism as a characteristic of feminist literary criticism, and indeed, this "method" has proved useful in connection with Welty's novels. Thus, in my study the term "female narrative strategies" is used in a broader sense: it embraces all those narrative devices that are indicative of female writing and that dissent from the dominant literary tradition. For each of the novels I have chosen an approach that is especially pertinent to the narrative structures of the particular novel.

The first chapter on Eudora Welty's first novel, *Delta Wedding*, is mainly a study in point of view. The basic assumption that a female author also engenders a female narrator will lead to the question of how this female narrator proceeds in her story. The theory of point of view by Susan Sniader Lanser[51] will be the theoretical basis for this chapter.

*The Golden Apples*[52] is teeming with allusions to myths. As mentioned above, the specific appropriation of the dominant language by women writers determines the discourse; thus, the story is new and different, too. The "new" versions of well-known stories or myths belonging to the canon of literature give especially ample evidence of this process. Christa Wolf, in her book *Kassandra*,[53] presents the figure of Cassandra from a new point of view, and in her lectures on the same topic she asks:

> Should we not once try to see what would happen if we placed women in the great patterns of world literature instead of men? Achilles, Heracles, Odysseus, Oedipus, Agamemnon, Jesus, King Lear, Faust, Julien Sorel, Wilhelm Meister.[54]

Welty's own short story "Circe" is such an attempt at presenting the female point of view of a classical myth by giving Circe a voice. Circe tells her own story about Odysseus's intrusion into her quiet life. Although at the end of the story Circe remains alone on her island, "sickened, with child,"[55] she nevertheless has her story; yes, we might even say that she takes away the story from Odysseus. In Margaret Atwood's "Circe/Mud Poems"[56] a similar process takes place. As in Welty's story, Circe is the first-person speaker, and she also describes herself as being abused by Odysseus. She even explicitly states that "It's the story that counts."[57] Alicia Suskin Ostriker's comment on Atwood's use of myths is also pertinent to Welty: "The poet simultaneously deconstructs a prior 'myth' or 'story' and constructs a new one which includes, instead of excluding, herself."[58]

Myths in works by women writers are frequently "revised" because they are retold from a new perspective. This revisionary perspective enables us to see and read new stories and question the old, canonical ones, which are always presented from a male perspective. I shall focus on the use of myths with regard to the female characters in *The Golden Apples* and comment on the "re-vision."[59]

In *Losing Battles*, which consists mainly of dialogues, aspects of the speech act theory provide a theoretical basis for an analysis of the speech acts of both female and male characters. The question in which respects the female protagonists divert from the norms of the community dominant in *Losing Battles* will also be considered.

Welty's last novel, *The Optimist's Daughter*, is a book about a daughter trying to come to terms with her dead parents. The issue of memory, together with the concept of time, will be analyzed in connection with a female experience. I will suggest that this novel is an example of a matrilinear narrative precisely because of the specifically female impact of memory.

A description of female narrative strategies enables the feminist critic to listen to the double-voiced discourse and to give meaning to the empty space.

## 2

# *Delta Wedding*: Point of View and Matriarchal Order

*Delta Wedding*, as its title implies, is a novel about a wedding taking place on a plantation in Mississippi in 1923. As in *Losing Battles*, where a birthday is the occasion for a family reunion, the family gathering for the wedding is the main event upon which the action of the novel centers. The bride and bridegroom are not the protagonists, but the bride's mother and sisters and their nine-year-old cousin Laura McRaven. Peggy Prenshaw points out that the Fairchild women dominate in the novel,[1] and it is indeed always a female perspective from which the story about Dabney Fairchild's wedding is presented. But the action in *Delta Wedding* does not convey the impression that the Fairchild family life is atypical of the traditional patriarchal family patterns especially dominant in plantation life.[2] The "grandly matriarchal order"[3] is established by a subtle, indirect way of depicting the frame of the wedding of the seventeen-year-old bride, who is on the brink of entering this patriarchal system as a wife. It is not the story that undermines this system, but the discourse with its implied modifications of the order of the action. The choice of an exclusively female point of view is bound to have effects on the presentation of the social order and its participants.

The main observer of the Fairchild world is cousin Laura. The fact that the third-person omniscient narrator often reveals the thoughts of a nine-year-old girl in connection with a wedding calls for particular attention. But the numerous shifts from Laura's point of view to the bride's, her mother's, and her sisters' also contribute to the diversity of a female point of view. The relation between story and discourse mentioned in my introduction helps to elucidate the dichotomy between the established patriarchal family system and the actual matriarchal order.

Analyzing the relation between story and discourse we realize how uneventful this novel is, or how little happens in *Delta Wedding*. Several early reviews of the novel refer to its lack of action or plot. One of the most outspoken critics in this respect is Diana Trilling. In her review in *The Nation* in 1946 she points out that "dramatically speaking, nothing happens in *Delta Wedding*."[4] However, this lack is counterbalanced by the descriptions of events taking place *within* the various female characters. As mentioned in the introduction, most of Welty's fiction is not plot oriented, but character oriented, and *Delta Wedding* is a case in point. The focus of the novel is on the presentation of a female response to the impending wedding, or rather on several responses, as the action is presented through the eyes of Laura, Dabney, Shelley, Robbie, and Ellen, "the mother of them all."[5] In this way the anticipation of a festive event is ever so subtly transformed into a critical portrayal of a seemingly idyllic life on a plantation in the Delta. At the time of its publication *Delta Wedding* was sometimes attacked because of its lack of social criticism, and Diana Trilling even spoke of its author as an "ingenious dreamer on the Southern past."[6] But the exclusively female point of view reveals that this plantation life bears all kinds of threats, dangers, and frustrations.

An analysis of point of view, especially of the dominant female point of view, demands an extensive apparatus of theoretical terms. In her poetics of point of view Susan Sniader Lanser tries to incorporate gender-based distinctions into her framework.[7] She points out that most narrative theorists refer to the narrator and writer as "he" and that they therefore subsume the woman writer under the male. It is necessary to view the conventions of literary communications in relation to the cultural norms to which writers recur; thus, the sex role system and its concepts of male and female play an important role. Lanser relies on aspects of speech act theory and on recent formalist/structuralist studies in order to create criteria for a theory of point of view which "can function at once as ideology and technique" (p. 63).[8] She establishes a comprehensive poetics of point of view, introducing three important categories, namely *status*, *contact*, and *stance*, which denote the speaker's or writer's relationship to the speech act, to the audience, and to the uttered message. These three categories are manifest in the fictional discourse; a description of them can give insight into the organization of point of view, which is

> a structural manifestation not only of aesthetic ideology but of the ideology of literary production itself. If we remember that ideology is not simply a content "poured into" the text but is the very fabric of textual organization, then we can recognize in point of view the potential for either obscuring or exposing its own ideological base. (p. 101)

Lanser insists on the relation between point of view and social structures: point of view reflects the structures of social life and its communicative activities. As the three categories *status*, *contact*, and *stance* mentioned above will prove quite useful in my more specific interpretations of the female point of view in *Delta Wedding*, I shall heavily rely on Lanser's definitions and explanations in the course of this chapter. Her concept of the poetics of point of view provides us with possibilities of investigating a narrator's or focalizer's status, contact, and stance in order to compare the text with the norms and conventions of its own time and place and compare the textual point of view with the literary activity that shaped it.

## INITIATION: LAURA AS AN ONLOOKER AT THE (DELTA) WEDDING

Like Frankie in McCullers's *The Member of the Wedding*, Laura is desperately trying to be part of her cousin's wedding. To participate in a wedding means to belong to a family, to follow a ritual, which in turn is constituted through a family. In *The Member of the Wedding* twelve-year-old Frankie undergoes the painful experience of becoming a woman while she witnesses the preparations for a wedding. She knows that her observations will refer to her own experience one day. Frankie vehemently refuses to accept the social norms around her, and she cannot cope with the options of American womanhood. The presentation of Laura does not focus on this painful knowledge, but the fact that we experience part of the preparation for the wedding through her eyes conveys the idea that Laura is a witness of a ritual basic to a woman's life. Furthermore, all female protagonists in *Delta Wedding* are presented as direct witnesses of the preparations for Dabney's wedding, whereas the men do not show much concern about the event, the bridegroom included. Their lives do not change, it seems, or at least the narrator does not consider it to be crucial enough to be reported. This indifference conveyed to us through the restricted or almost nonexistent male point of view throws light on the gender-determined society and its rigid patriarchal pattern, especially dominant in the South of the twenties. Laura at her age already knows that

> it was the boys and the men that defined that family always. All the girls knew it. When she looked at the boys and the men Laura was without words but she knew that company like a dream that comes back again and again, each aspect familiar and longing not to be forgotten. Great-Great-Uncle George on his horse, in his portrait in the parlor . . . even he, she had learned by looking up at him, had the family trait of quick, upturning smiles, instant comprehension of the smallest eddy of life in the current of the day, which would surely be entered in a kind of reckless pleasure. This pleasure either the young men copied from the older ones or the older ones always kept. (p. 14)

The narrator's ideological stance[9] seems to coincide with the cultural norms; in other words, the patriarchal pattern is presented as the norm. Yet, the fact that Laura experiences this male supremacy as paralyzing—she is without words—questions this male dominance. Thus, on the axis of coincidence according to Lanser the culture text is opposed. "Culture text" is borrowed from Juri Lotman and is defined as "the world view operating in a given time and place" (Lanser, p. 56). Furthermore, only the reader knows about Laura's ambivalent attitude towards these male norms, and the intimacy created by this knowledge enforces the reader's sympathy for Laura. This privileged relationship between the protagonist, the narrator, and the reader contributes to the questioning of the culture text because the reader tends to take Laura's side.

The rigid patriarchal system alluded to in the quotation is related to the theme of change. Laura is extraordinarily susceptible to change, and the narrator tells us that "Laura from her earliest memory had heard how they [the Fairchilds] 'never seemed to change at all' " (p. 15). Now, all the family members are included, "boys and men, girls and ladies all, the old and the young of the Delta kin—even the dead and the living, for Aunt Shannon—were alike—no gap opened between them" (p. 14). The likeness between them also implies a quality of timelessness, of the never-changing family structure of the Fairchilds. Yet, Laura is aware of a change going on in all of them, in spite of the rigidness and constancy: "The outside did not change but the inside did" (p. 15). At the very beginning of the novel the change of "the inside" is presented as being crucial to Laura: her mother had died some months ago, and she now lives alone with her father. She is on her first trip by herself, looking forward to spending some time with her mother's relatives. Everything seems to be moving: the train, of course, bringing Laura; the butterflies flying in and out of the windows of the train; fragrances of flowers and woods; the lamp in the train swinging on a chain. Change also awaits Laura at Shellmound plantation: the marriage between Dabney and Troy the overseer will certainly bring some change to the Fairchild family. The more Laura senses that "they changed every moment" (p. 15), the more alertly she watches her surroundings. Perceptive of change, she is introduced to secrets she would not get acquainted with at her home in Jackson.

Laura's status as a visitor from a different place contributes to her position as onlooker. As Douglas Messerli points out, "as an outsider Laura is very much aware of time and the separation from loved ones that time can cause, a heavy burden of awareness for a nine year old."[10] Time,[11] here, is undoubtedly linked with change and separation; in Laura's case it means above all final separation from her beloved mother. Therefore, Laura is most sensitive to time, and past and present are always with her: she "remembered everything" (p. 7). Her memory determines her attitude towards the present, and she does not try to forget or idealize the past as Laurel does at the beginning of *The Optimist's Daughter* till she realizes that memory must be "vulnerable to the living moment" (*OD*, p. 179).[12] Some of the Fairchilds are also able to perceive the flux of time, but in general they live for the present ("even Laura's arrival today was past now," p. 15) and they never seem to remember things (cf.

p. 134).[13] Thus, Laura is surrounded by people who are quite different from her and yet try to make her feel at home and protected since she is a "little motherless girl" (p. 3). Indeed, the Fairchilds introduce Laura—the onlooker[14] and outsider—to a new life. The names Mc*Raven* and *Fair*child also reflect the difference between her character and that of the host family. She is the dark girl from a place the others do not care about.

We would expect that Laura's journey to the Fairchild plantation includes meetings with people who know more than she does and who are able and willing to communicate that knowledge to her. The journey, which is traditionally linked with a quest of a young hero, also initiates Laura into a new realm of existence and provides her with insights. But contrary to a male hero's initiating journey, it does not necessitate adventures such as struggling with nature, exploring new land, fighting an enemy (often a red Indian). All these activities are especially pertinent to American male heroes who grow to maturity and search for identity with the help of an older mate.[15] Initiation often means acquaintance with something that enables human beings to have insights into a new realm of existence.

For Laura, the Fairchilds partly function as helpmates in order to gain these insights. Yet, among them there are gradual and conspicuous differences in sensibility and knowledge, and they all contribute to Laura's initiation in different ways. Ellen, the mother of Laura's cousins, is the figure who is closest to Laura's emotional state. She is also an outsider; she has been one since the day she left her home in Virginia. Ellen does not knowingly initiate Laura into a new life. It is partly through their emotional kinship that Laura learns from Ellen about the peculiarities of a Fairchild woman.

But it is also Laura herself who acquires knowledge through her own observations of the new surroundings. Only because of her imagination can she both witness and sympathize with events that nobody explains to her. She is endowed with an imagination that she might have inherited from her mother. A crucial experience in her life and memory was her mother's ability to create a doll for Laura out of stockings. It was her mother's imagination that made her use whatever was available at that very moment and that fulfilled her daughter's wish. Laura definitely knows that she will never have this "instant answer to a wish, for her mother was dead" (p. 233). This insight is important for her because it influences her still childlike attitude towards wishes. Significantly, her nine-year-old cousin India expresses a wish and hopes for immediate fulfillment as well (cf. p. 27). Although India finds out things "like magic" (p. 105), she is still the protected child of the Fairchild family, whereas Laura senses that she can no longer rely on such a protection. Therefore she must view her surroundings more observantly. Her observations are frequently presented through her point of view. We can say that the process of initiation is directly linked with point of view.

Laura's relationship to the Fairchild family illustrates her ambiguous position. She wants to be loved and cared for, and at the same time she yearns for independence and separateness. For example, she loves to read in her bed in the morning and hates being disturbed by Dabney pulling her out of bed. Or she resents the family's manifest desire to prevent her from thinking of her mother. The constant busy occupations on Shellmound plantation make it hard for Laura to decide on her own ways. Like the rest of the family she is taken in by this bustling atmosphere. She cannot express her own needs explicitly, but in her mind she is much more specific about her preferences and dislikes. She apprehends that she is waiting for something her heart craves for, yet that "the answer to the heart's pull" (p. 76) has not come so far.

Laura as focalizer informs us about her inner desires; the explanation given indicates that her waiting and yearning is connected with her gender:

> She imagined that one day—maybe the next, in the Fairchild house—she would know the answer to the heart's pull, just as it would come to her in school why the apple was pulled down on Newton's head, and that it was the way for girls in the world that they should be put off, put off, put off—and told a little later; but told, surely. (p. 76)

The presentation of Laura's consciousness is typical of the double-voiced discourse: a girl's or woman's wish is expressed, its negation or restriction of fulfillment immediately follows, and a more general statement about a convention regarding girls or women is added. It is not explicitly stated that the restriction has its roots in the gender of the character; on the contrary, the statement sounds like a corroboration of an accepted convention. A lack or illusion is explained by a gender convention. But the fact that it is mentioned from the perspective of the female, who is painfully experiencing it, and the fact that it occurs so frequently in a novel in which so little happens, stresses the contradiction between the female's state of mind and the convention reflected by the status quo. We can speak of a questioning of cultural norms, which the narrator's ideological stance evokes. The narrator's ideological stance obviously does not coincide with the culture text, otherwise the contradiction would not be so consistent throughout the novel.

Another narrative concept, narrative status, also throws light on a typically gender-based experience. As mentioned above, the narrative status is linked with the narrator's involvement in the story. In the following example the narrator does not enter Laura's mind but chooses to report certain impressions of hers that definitely reveal a female narrative voice. Since we have a heterodiegetic voice we would expect the narrator to have access to information concerning all the characters, but it is conspicuous that the narrator limits herself to information about the female character. Lanser's axis of privilege with its poles "human limitation" and "omniscience" (Lanser, p. 161) in this respect is useful to demonstrate that our narrator can be placed in between these two poles because she is much more restricted to the female characters, that is, in our example, to Laura. This significant episode in Laura's encounter with a gender-determined society takes place on the river Yazoo, the "River of Death" (p. 194): without a warning Laura is thrown into the river by her cousin Roy. He fishes her out when he realizes that Laura would drown, although he "thought girls floated" (p. 179).[16] Laura's experience in the water vividly illustrates how she is faced with an aggressive act coming from a representative of the male sex.

The description of Laura's frightening experience underwater bears traces of a sexual initiation that she undergoes as an unprotected girl:

> As though Aunt Studney's sack had opened after all, like a whale's mouth, Laura opening her eyes head down saw its insides all around her—dark water and fearful fishes. A face flanked by receding arms looked at her under water—Roy's, a face strangely indignant and withdrawing. Then Roy's legs drove about her—she saw Roy's tied-up toe, knew his foot, and seized hold. He kicked her, then his unfamiliar face again met hers, wide-eyed and small-mouthed and its hair streaming upwards, and his hands took her by her hair and pulled her up like a turnip. (p. 178)

Roy's dehumanized, almost monsterlike face between the "fearful fishes" appears to Laura as something threatening, unknown, and ungraspable. The sexual dimension is enhanced by the reference to Aunt Studney's sack, from which, as Roy has informed Laura previously, Ellen gets her babies. Laura is fascinated by this idea and wishes to look into this mysterious sack. In Joyce's *Ulysses* Stephen Dedalus is equally attracted by a "midwife's bag" and imagines its contents. His thoughts range from the naval cord, to his mother's womb, and finally to the sexual act.[17] Aunt Studney's sack, resembling "a whale's mouth," is suggestive of death and (re)birth similar to Tashtego's experience in *Moby Dick*. The dark water enclosing Laura is compared to the inside of the sack, but Laura is not ready for this "knowledge"; on the contrary, she is horrified by the sudden plunge into this unknown realm. It is illustrative to refer to the stronger sexual imagery of this river episode in the unpublished short story "The Delta Cousins," where an old "beeman" exposes himself to Laura and India. Laura perceives the man's genitals as "a little old fish"[18] coming out of the man's trousers. In the novel the experience of a nine-year-old girl confronted with the realm of sexuality, unknown to her so far, is depicted through a series of more allusive fear-inspiring images. Laura shows traits of a victimlike object that must yield to the male's rescuing action: "he pulled her out, arm by arm and leg by leg, and set her up in the boat" (p. 178).[19] Although Laura grasps Roy by his foot, she is still presented as the victim; the description "arm by arm and leg by leg" connoting fragmentation emphasizes Laura's state as victim in this initiation process.

The hidden and veiled references to Laura's vulnerability and exposure in connection with sexuality continue even after the boat episode: at home she realizes that she has lost a pin that belonged to Ellen and that Laura had found together with Roy. This pin has symbolic value for Ellen since it is a present from her husband, Battle, before their marriage.[20] Ellen has had a dream in which she has found the pin. The loss of the pin by Laura in the Yazoo River viewed within this context and the metaphorical sexual implications of the boat episode refer to some loss of Laura's innocence: metaphorically she has had a glimpse of the inside of Aunt Studney's sack, but this "insight" has also left her bereft of a "treasure" (p. 179).[21]

The depiction of this boat experience obviously concentrates on Laura's gender: the narrator uses a train of events that, viewed as a whole, makes us realize how gender-specific the narrative stance is. Significantly, through the narrator's ideological stance the reader's sympathy for Laura's experience is aroused because the reader is confronted with a presentation of Laura's helpless floating from her perspective, and the reader experiences it with her. The girl, exposed to the boy's (phallic) power, is a representative of the ("weaker") sex, which is traditionally a target of this power. The ideological narrative stance questions the notion of these discriminating conditions and patterns.

In her essay on cultural patterns in *Delta Wedding*, Peggy Prenshaw points out that the conventions valid on Shellmound plantation are characteristic of southern culture: they underlie the agrarian life with its "dependence on the seasons as a regulatory force on one's life, the isolation from the world at large, the family unity, and the strong ties to the land and to a sense of history."[22] Prenshaw's comment on the dependence on nature is crucial in the sense that the female characters in *Delta Wedding* have a more passionate relation to nature than the men. They are aware of nature's cycles, they smell the fragrances of flowers and trees, they enjoy its beauty, they *know* nature. Dabney, wondering what she knows, realizes that "she could see a single leaf on a willow tree as far as the bayou's edge, such clarity as there was in everything" (p. 90). Ellen's love and responsibility for her garden, which she is afraid to leave when she would be giving birth to her ninth child, is characteristic of the attitude many fictional female characters have. Like Elisa in Steinbeck's "Chrysanthemums," Ellen feels that her flowers represent a domain where nobody should or can interfere with or dominate her. For Shelley the line of trees at Shellmound is persistent; the confinement she experiences there is expressed by the image of the tree: "Why are you thinking your line of trees the indelible thing in the world?" (p. 219). The men in *Delta Wedding* only express their concern about nature's cycles when their corn or grain is threatened. Otherwise, a male response to nature is hardly mentioned.

The dominant female response to nature in *Delta Wedding* brings other examples by women writers to mind. One of the best-known and most striking examples of this intense relation to nature is the description in *The Mill on the Floss* when Maggie decides to visit the "Hill." There she enjoys the "free air" and is charmed by the old fir tree.[23] Edna Pontellier in Kate Chopin's *The Awakening* is overwhelmed when she is standing naked under the sky, and then, swimming far out in the sea, remembers "the hum of the bees and the musky odor of pinks"[24] of her childhood. Eudora Welty's Delta, by night looking "just like a big bed, the whiteness in the luminous dark" (p. 239), bears traits of the "female landscape" with "the upswelling land" that Ellen Moers speaks of.[25] Furthermore, the name "Shellmound" also suggests a female realm. Westling points out that one of the Indian mounds, which are typical of the Delta landscape, is called "The Great Mother."[26]

This conspicuous difference between male and female characters with respect to nature is also pertinent to "the isolation from the world at large," and to the ways in which the characters (male and female) resort to their inner lives. John Edward Hardy explains that their lives are not only "intensely private—but . . . they are ritualistic too."[27] For Hardy the rituals at Shellmound belong to cultural patterns, therefore they "transcend the privacy"[28] of the characters. This observation is crucial, because it means that the privacy and inner seclusion of the female characters belong to an order that encompasses more than just that of a girl or woman on a southern plantation in the twenties. It reflects a way of thinking and feeling typical of the common expectations of a woman's role. I suggest that John Edward Hardy's comment on this inner privacy is especially true for the female characters. Laura, the nine-year-old, already knows that she must keep things to herself, and Shelley expresses this attitude quite explicitly: "Women, she was glad to think, did know a *little* better—though everything they knew they would have to keep to themselves . . . oh, forever" (p. 196).

Thus, in *Delta Wedding*, the narrative strategy demonstrates the opposite of what the female characters actually perform. The predominant female point of view and the exploring of the female characters' inner selves give evidence that the narrator obviously wishes to break the "silence," even if only on the narratological level. The social identity of the third-person narrator, who is not a character in the novel, is related to the author's female social identity because of literary conventions; thus, we presume the narrator to be female. The contact between the narrator and the narratee[29] is established by the general statement the narrator makes about women. Approaching the problem of the narrator's identity, Lanser enumerates a list of aspects that determine social identity, among which she names gender as "the most universally central to *linguistic* activity in Western culture" (Lanser, p. 166) because of the gender distinctions in Indo-European languages. In cultural communication gender is responsible for sex differences in everyday life: "sex is important to the encoding and decoding of narrative voice" p. 166). The following example by Lanser illustrates narrative conventions that reflect gender-determined thinking: in a text not explicitly marked as written by a male author, we presume a male authorship, and only if we come across a female name on the title page do we expect a female narrative voice.

Laura's decision not to tell the Fairchilds that "in the end she would go—go from all this" (p. 237) is indicatory of the awareness that one knows better but had rather not tell the others, even if they are close relatives. It is not coincidental that the narrator uses the word "secret" for this awareness of Laura's: keeping a "secret" in *Delta Wedding* is entirely restricted to the female character. Significantly, they do not do it out of secretiveness but out of knowledge. Experience must have taught them not to confide in others.

These experiences proper are seldom described, but they are implicitly present because of the above-mentioned forms of behavior of the female characters, who cannot put sufficient confidence into their surroundings. Not even Ellen seems to trust her husband, since she keeps all her worries and thoughts to herself. Dabney, the bride, is also reticent and does not let her future husband know her thoughts and expectations of marriage.

The narrative stance with its relationship between the narrator's personality and values and the culture text illustrates how a cultural convention is indirectly questioned. Especially Laura's dissatisfaction with certain gender conventions is voiced through the narrator, who still uses her own language and presents it by stating a more or less general observation. Laura's experience of being initiated into the life at Shellmound is mainly determined by her growing awareness of the restricted gender conventions.

## DABNEY: ADOLESCENT AND BRIDE

At seventeen Dabney is still a young girl, but already a bride. Even for the twenties she is extremely young to get married. Her future husband Troy is thirty-four; as the overseer of the plantation he is socially below Dabney, a fact nobody is enthusiastic about but nobody would admit openly. Dabney is aware that she is acting against her family's will, but she has no resentment; on the contrary, she even feels proud of her disagreement.

Dabney's relationship to Troy is not very emotional and deep; they hardly know each other. "She really noticed him first—last summer" (p. 30), when he was on horseback. Now, a few days before the wedding, Dabney feels that "he still charm[s] her most" (p. 30) when there is a distance between them.

Marriage for Dabney, it seems, is a way to get away from the daily routine and to have a "solid house" (p. 90) of her own. Yet, Dabney does not marry out of sheer desire to be protected. There is a rebellious strain in her, too, which probably triggered off her decision to marry Troy. She likes the idea of her father disagreeing with her choice of a husband: "It would kill her father" (p. 33). This knowledge fills her with triumph, which can be interpreted as a slight revenge on her father, who shares certain characteristics with the omniscient authoritative patriarch.[30]

The narrator tells us very little about the reasons for Dabney's wish to marry Troy. We receive some insights into Dabney's thinking indirectly: the narrator describes Dabney's visit to Marmion, her future home, before the wedding. She is terrified when she realizes that this house once belonged to her grandfather, who was killed in a duel to decide a point of honor. Dabney knows that at that time honor had something to do with cotton, but to her "all the cotton in the world was not worth one moment of life" (pp. 120–121). This scene reflects a characteristic pattern of southern history and culture: the past catches up with Dabney, who no longer accepts the values of these former times.[31] Already as a little girl she denied them when the boys told the story of the duel shouting " 'Bang bang!' " (p. 122). Such a seemingly unimportant reference to a childhood event can create an awareness in the reader of differing concepts of history between the sexes.

After Dabney's remembrance of her grandfather and his southern code of honor the focus shifts to the surroundings of the house. This shift is a common device in Welty's narrative style: inner events of female characters are frequently connected with descriptions of nature. Indeed, these descriptions even interrupt the reflections and introduce another kind of reflection. The description of the sun lighting the house triggers off Dabney's thoughts about her childhood and at the same time refers to an anticipated future. The instant present of the light introduces the darker past, but also puts her new house into a "lighter" perspective. In her classification of narrative modes for presenting consciousness in fiction Dorrit Cohn comments on the use of the narrated monologue: "The narrated monologue is a choice medium for revealing a fictional mind suspended in an instant present, between a remembered past and an anticipated future."[32] The narrated monologue is a means Welty often uses to reveal a character's, especially a female's, mind, but she maintains the third-person voice. Many male writers dealing with male adolescence "adopt the adolescent response to experience" and often write in a fragmentary kind of prose that is a combination of "factual accuracy and blurred emotional fervour."[33] Welty uses quite a different narrative strategy: she combines the narrated monologue with descriptions of nature. Moreover, they function as a link between narrated monologues with different themes. The narrated monologue combined with descriptions of natural surroundings is a narrative strategy used predominantly by women writers. Virginia Woolf's *The Waves* is a case in point, although the narrated monologues between the nature descriptions are much longer, more extensive, and multifarious. But the nature descriptions beginning with "the sun" also metaphorically illuminate the narrated monologues. The metaphorical meaning of the sun is especially used to elucidate the growing and then gradually diminishing awareness of consciousness in the psyche of the first-person narrator.[34] Welty's characterization of Dabney is achieved by a similar use of narrative strategy: the hints of reticence indicated by shifts in Dabney's reflective mood combined with the nature descriptions underscore her insecure situation. She, the bride of the Delta wedding, is characterized by her tentative attempt to express her expectations of her future married life.

The night-light that Dabney has received as a wedding present from her aunts and that she breaks carrying home is obviously a metaphor of loss and even of death. The night-light once belonged to her Aunt Mashula, who waited for her husband to return from the Civil War "till the lightning one early morning stamped her picture on the window-pane" (p. 45). It also stands for the inevitable link with the past that Dabney tries to cut off. Since she breaks the night-light before she has ever used it, we could say that she closes her eyes before this past without trying to understand it. It is noteworthy that Eudora Welty uses the china night-light as an example in her essay "Place in Fiction" to illustrate how a "good novel" should work.[35] The lamp she mentions is the same as in *Delta Wedding*: it shows a view of a town (in the essay it is London) on the outside, and if the lamp is lit, the town seems to be on fire: "The lamp alight is the combination of internal and external, glowing at the imagination as one" (*ES*, p. 120). The scene is thus illuminated by the candle, or, figuratively, by the story-teller, the writer. Breaking the light implies that this effect cannot be produced, the internal and external do not merge. Indeed, Dabney instinctively realizes that she has lost something irreparable. George, the member of the Fairchild family who is the least tied to the past, significantly presumes that Dabney will never miss "a little old piece of glass" (p. 53).[36]

We will later see that the image of light is also linked with time, whose influence Dabney's elder sister Shelley recognizes but Dabney does not. Barbara MacKenzie elaborates on this relationship between light and time in Welty's work. MacKenzie uses *One Time, One Place* to illustrate that both in a photographer's vision and a writer's vision "light glares and burns and shines; it is life-giving; it casts shadows; it outlines." For a photographer and a writer "images of light . . . are related intimately with time, for seasons affect the quality of light, as does time of day."[37] Dabney's marriage to Troy is an escape from time in the past, but an escape to something that is breakable as well. The broken night-light will never illuminate her married life with Troy. In this respect John Edward Hardy sees the "themes of protection and disaster . . . inextricably bound up together from the first,"[38] and I agree with his observation that the past and present always appear together. From Dabney, though, we do not get much information about her anticipated future and her hope for protection as Troy's wife. Metaphorically, on the level of point of view, the internal view of Dabney is not possible because the night-light is broken entirely. The external view only provides the reader with partial "visibility" (cf. *ES*, p. 120).

## SHELLEY: THE YOUNG WOMAN

The first scene in which the reader learns more about Shelley is significantly observed by Laura as well. Laura sneeks to her room and, standing in the door, watches Shelley writing in her diary. The reader can look over Shelley's shoulder and read her private thoughts, whereas Laura will never know what Shelley confides to her diary. Yet, Shelley and Laura's concerns about love in general and love in the family are similar.

Shelley's room is indicative of her inner life: it reflects a very private self. There are many things on display on her desk: the jars with last year's roses, which still preserve their perfume and which Shelley loves to smell. There are photographs from past years, a little box from one of her aunts, in short, numerous little things that are meaningful to nobody else but Shelley. The leaves with last year's perfume are significant for Shelley's attitude towards the past: it is for her, as Douglas Messerli puts it, "not completed, finished, dead, but is something living and forceful because it shapes the present, defines it."[39] Shelley's urge to write in her diary gives evidence of her belief in the power and influence of past events. By writing down her thoughts and ideas with respect to past events she implicitly states the significance of the moment, of the present in relation to the past. Whatever Shelley writes down is a fusion of past events and of the moment, of the here and now. In *The Optimist's Daughter* the interrelation between past and present is more radically expressed through memory, whereas in Shelley's case the reflections of the moment dominate the issues treated in the diary.

Shelley is very much concerned with the approaching wedding. Dabney and Troy seem to be on her mind frequently, and her thoughts about the two trigger off all kinds of associations mainly dealing with her family's problems. She does not believe in the security and togetherness of the Fairchild family:

> We never wanted to be smart, one by one, but all together we have a wall, we are self-sufficient against people that come up knocking, we are solid to the outside. Does the world suspect? that we are all very private people? I think one by one we're all more lonely than private and more lonely than self-sufficient. . . . I feel we should all be cherished but not all together in a bunch—separately, but not one to go unloved for the other loved. (p. 84)

Shelley is suspicious of the seemingly idyllic way of life on the plantation. She realizes that in the last resort human beings are separate and isolated, in spite of the outward appearance of the Fairchild clan. Indeed, Shelley expresses a predicament that is a central theme in Welty's fiction. In his famous article on "The Love and the Separateness in Miss Welty," Robert Penn Warren mentions isolation and alienation as the basic issues in Welty's fiction.[40] Shelley's private act of writing in her diary and expressing this isolation emphasizes her particular separation from the Fairchild family.[41] Writing in a diary establishes a more intimate relationship between the reader and Shelley: the third-person narrator is hardly involved here. In Lanser's terminology, this contact between reader and the first person is called "overt." While an "I" narrator establishes overt contact, other narrators may not make contact at all. Several axes of the narrator's contact are set up by Lanser (e.g., "narrative self-consciousness" versus "narrative unconsciousness," or "confidence" versus "uncertainty") (Lanser, pp. 177–179). With regard to Shelley we can say that within the narrated world a narrative self-consciousness is expressed. Writing in a diary is a nonpublic speech act, and it is typical of Shelley's silent rebellion.

As a female adolescent Shelley is very much aware of the

patriarchal pressures around her. The violent (male) plantation world especially frightens her when she witnesses a quarrel between Troy and a black worker. The black man holds an ice pick drawn, while Troy searches for his gun. Troy shoots at a finger of the black man's hand. Shelley reluctantly leaves Troy's office because she can hardly bear walking through a door on which there is blood. Thus, jumping over the door sill, she feels that "[n]obody could marry a man with blood on his door" (p. 196). Running back home she angrily asks herself whether all men (cf. p. 196) imitate other men, her father included. Shelley looks back to the past again, recognizing some universal truths in the behavior of the men dominating the Delta. She concludes that men are not much different from little children, while women know "a *little* better—though everything they knew they would have to keep to themselves" (p. 196). Shelley's act of writing into her diary is an example of this secret attitude: she expresses her anger, fear, and disillusionment in her diary. Yet, at some moments she ardently speaks out against the suppressing surroundings. A striking example of female rebellion is her accusation that her father is responsible for her mother's tenth pregnancy, which Shelley calls a "predicament" (p. 229).

But in general Shelley keeps her private self protected from the Fairchild clan, and we can hardly imagine how she will ever break out of her world the way she does in her diary. Hers is an imaginary world. Her decision never to get married (cf. p. 136) is part of her rebellious stance, but we have our doubts whether she will not live a life similar to her aunts', which is as narrow and restricted as her own family's. Shelley's fear of this world gives evidence of threatening powers in the midst of this seemingly idyllic world of the Fairchilds:

> A big beetle, a horned one, was trying to get in. All at once Shelley was sickeningly afraid of life, life itself, afraid *for* life. . . . (p. 197)

In connection with the preparations for a wedding it is significant that both Shelley and Laura express their reluctance to get married.[42] Their mutual doubts regarding marriage illustrate their awareness of the restriction they might experience. This attitude is bound to attract the reader's attention since this novel is about a wedding. The ideological narrative stance of this text questions the culture text because Shelley and Laura as predominant focalizers indirectly express a different ideology. Ideological stance deals with the authority of a text, which is dependent on the emphasis given to the stance and on the importance of the persona that takes the stance. Isolated ideology and reinforced ideology are the poles of this axis. The most fully reinforced ideology is being conveyed if more than one voice and more than one way (e.g., the story's outcome and narrative comments) reveal it. Moreover, if the position of the persona uttering a particular stance is rather dominant in the narrative structure, he or she has more authority. Thus, authorial narrators usually demonstrate more authority than fictional characters, and focalizers have more authority than nonfocalizers. When there are several voices on the same level it is possible to distinguish between a more dominant voice and a subordinate voice. The authority of our text depends on the emphasis attributed to the ideological narrative stance and on focalizing characters such as Laura and Shelley.

## ELLEN: THE EARTH MOTHER FIGURE

Like Laura, Ellen is an outsider amongst the Fairchilds, although she is "the mother of them all"[43] (p. 10). Before she came to Shellmound, she had been a schoolteacher in Virginia.[44] Another crucial attitude she shares with Laura is her awareness of time and her knowledge of what a moment can mean in one's life and how a moment can bring about change, especially through love, birth, and death.

> No, she had never had time—much time at all, to contemplate . . . but she knew. Well, one moment told

> you the great things, one moment was enough for you to know the greatest things. (p. 240)

In her essay "Some Notes on Time in Fiction," Welty speaks of time as "the bringer-on of action, the instrument of change,"[45] and it is indeed this aspect of change Ellen senses and recognizes. Being "the mother of them all," she frequently is overloaded with work, commitments, and responsibility. Ironically, she who is susceptibly aware of time often runs against it. She desperately tries to find some time to work in her garden in order to prevent it from becoming a wilderness. In spite of the fact that "she never actually had time to sit down and fill her eyes with people and hear what they said, in any civilized way" (p. 221), Ellen's capacity to observe the people around her, perceive their problems, and react towards their need for love is conspicuous. Moreover, beauty and harmony affect her deeply.

Her encounter with a strange girl in the woods leaves a vivid impression on her. She is immediately drawn to this extremely beautiful girl: "A whole mystery of life opened up" (p. 70). The girl stands still in a way none of her daughters ever did, and Ellen reflects whether she has ever hoped for this beauty when asking her children to stand still. Ellen is perceptive of this moment of stillness and beauty.[46] Ellen Moers points out that in Woolf's *To the Lighthouse* Mrs. Ramsay is also one of these mothers who is painfully aware of the moment and who "make of the moment something permanent."[47] It is not coincidental that Mrs. Ramsay, too, asks her son James to stand still,[48] expressing a motherly wish. They are mothers, troubled by their daily commitments, yet intensely susceptible to the meaning of a moment, of beauty.

For Ellen the beautiful girl also conveys something inexplicable, something she cannot account for. Indeed, the girl appears like a faun in the woods or, rather, as his female counterpart, Fauna, who represents the spirit of the countryside and fertility. If we think of the Greek equivalent,

Pan, who is connected with sex, the symbolic apparition of this girl is even more intelligible since she herself is also associated with sex. George, the male Fairchild outsider, has encountered the girl and made love to her shortly before Ellen meets her. When George tells Ellen about his encounter, she is at first startled and upset and immediately thinks of her own daughter Dabney, who is about the same age as the mysterious girl. Her maternal feelings surge up within her and finally encompass the whole family:

> She had feared for the whole family, somehow, at a time like this (being their mother, and the atmosphere heavy with the wedding and the festivities hanging over their heads) when this girl, that was at first so ambiguous, and so lovely even to her all dull and tired—when she touched at their life, ran through the woods. (p. 80)

Ellen's acknowledgment of vulnerability is typically female in the sense that it is evoked by her realization that the beautiful, lonely girl is liable to a man's approaches, in spite of the fact that this man is her beloved and admired brother-in-law. It is significant that at the reception after the wedding ceremony the photographer announces the death of this girl; walking on the railroad track she was killed by the train. Again it is Ellen's emotional reaction we get: she has "a vision of fate" (p. 218). Albert J. Devlin refers to a similar situation in Woolf's *Mrs. Dalloway*, when Mrs. Dalloway learns of Septimus's tragic death.[49] In both cases only the two women are shown as being deeply affected by the sad news and they are both engaged in a social event (wedding reception, party).

Welty's subtle narrative strategy expressing a typically female experience is indicative of the hidden patterns which determine the lives of the Shellmound women. The narrator would never give an explicit critical statement on the situation of women, but the structure of the discursive presentation of events and the dialogues between certain characters convey information which is essential for our deeper understanding of the characters, of which women play the important parts. It is only through the narrative strategy that the reader comes to realize that the depiction of Southern life in Shellmound neither lacks social criticism nor is "morally discriminating" as has been stated by some critics.[50] In her review Diana Trilling speaks out harshly against Welty's presentation of an idyllic plantation life:

> As I say, it is where "Delta Wedding" implies—and the implication is pervasive—that the parochialism and snobbery of the Fairchild clan is the condition of the Fairchild kind of relaxation and charm, or that the Fairchild grace has a necessary source in a life of embattled pride, that I must deeply oppose its values.[51]

Readers like Trilling underestimate the various allusions and references to loneliness, fears, threats, dangers, and even death, which predominantly occur in relation to the female characters. Furthermore, a comment by the narrator such as the following questions the "embattled pride" of the Fairchilds: "But she was tired, and sometimes now the whole world seemed rampant, running away from her, and she would always be carrying another child to bring into it" (p. 78). This comment is part of the above-mentioned critical presentation of women's lives on a well-to-do southern plantation of the twenties.[52] Especially Ellen, who seems to be an ideal mother-figure in the novel, must be conceived with regard to the subtext. Marginal events such as the dialogue between her and George on the beautiful girl are covered up as being essential for the possibility of a female world other than the one presented by the surface of the text or the so-called empty space. The lack of plot and character development in *Delta Wedding* has a meaning that can only be detected and can only make sense in relation to the "schizoid perspective"[53] of the female text.

## NARRATOR AND MALE CHARACTERS

Battle and George Fairchild and Troy Flavin, Dabney's bridegroom, are the men belonging to the Fairchild community. The omniscient narrator never provides us with any insights into their inner lives. Instead, we catch glimpses of their characteristics through the eyes of some of the female characters.

We hardly get to know Battle Fairchild, the head of the plantation. When he is focused on, he is presented as the authoritarian patriarch in spite of the seemingly women-dominated Fairchild world. Almost all the descriptions of Battle express his tendency to exercise power and to show determination. Again, this characteristic is not articulated in a straightforward way by the narrator. The relation between the social context and the descriptive observation is established by the concatenation of certain attributes. The first description refers to Battle as a man with "his planter's boots creaking under the table when he stood to carve the turkeys" (p. 11). The chosen attributes belong to the plantation owner who gives orders and is used to obedience. It is not surprising that after this first description Laura immediately remembers that Battle was the one who did not let his children remain left-handed. Ellen also recalls Battle's stern attitude and tremulously recalls her husband's "determined breaking of her children's left-handedness" (p. 23).

Troy Flavin, the plantation overseer who marries into the Fairchild family, is mostly seen through the eyes of his future wife, Dabney. But we learn more about Dabney than about Troy when the narrator enters Dabney's mind. Troy himself never reveals why he wants to marry Dabney; it seems as if the narrator is not interested in the bridegroom of the Delta wedding. Only during one conversation with Ellen does he tell us something about himself. Typically enough, it is Ellen who makes him open up his heart about his mother, his house, and the hills he comes from. The narrator explicitly states that a man like Battle "would never have asked a man such a thing" (p. 94). This comment is an example of how the narrator chooses the questions a *woman* might ask. The narrator is aware of gender differences and of their effect on the contents of such a conversation. The following piece of dialogue between Ellen and Troy reflects a similar gender-determined attitude:

> "You were an only child? Like me?" she said . . .
>
> "Only boy."
>
> Ellen could not imagine a boy not enumerating his sisters, but she nodded. (p. 94)

Apart from such indirect information about Troy conveying a rather narrow mind, the reader gains the impression that Troy is not much interested in human relationships and that he considers women to be completely unimportant for the family structure.

George, Battle's brother, is the most interesting male character in the novel. Vande Kieft calls him the hero of the novel because he is presented through the eyes of Laura, Dabney, Shelley, and Ellen.[54] They are all impressed by his special way of keeping himself apart from the Fairchild clan (he does not live on Shellmound plantation; he has married Robbie, a local store clerk). In the eyes of the female observers mentioned above he seems to be the only one capable of true love. This love is for example manifest in the way he has thrown himself on the trestle in order to save his niece Maureen and thus has put his life at stake; or, Dabney remembers admiringly how he separated two black boys fighting. Like Laura, Dabney, and Shelley, Ellen realizes that George has a specific way of relating to people. When she learns about his encounter with the strange girl she is at first terrified but then struck by his honesty and seriousness; he does not hide his weaknesses or make jokes about them as some of the Fairchilds do. Since the omniscient third-person narrator focuses on George through Ellen, the reader again gains insight into Ellen's inner life: she or he even learns that Ellen is attracted to George.

Through multiple focalization of the female characters on the male characters the women take over some of the omniscience of the third-person narrator. According to Lanser's terminology they are focalizers while the narrator's voice is narrating. The narrative consciousness "receives" the focalizers' perceptions, thoughts, and feelings.[55] Laura, Dabney, Shelley, Ellen, and even Robbie all convey a woman's point of view, but each with her particular background and story. What they share is their awareness that they cannot fully accept the Fairchild solidarity. In this respect George has a catalyzing effect; he also refuses to be part of the seemingly secure and stable Fairchild world. The women characters sense the deviating tendency in George and in themselves. They observe and notice it because George lives accordingly, but they keep their own fears and doubts about the vulnerability of the Fairchild world to themselves. They are "active" in the sense that they observe and *see*, and that their thoughts are conveyed to us. From a narrator's point of view, George and the other two male characters are passive, i.e., the narrator does not seem to enter their minds and let them be focalizers.

The relation between the narrator and the male characters can be viewed in a broader context. In *Delta Wedding* the culture of the post–World War I South is depicted. Since we are confronted with the women's perspectives exclusively, with their emphasis on distance and separateness, we experience the southern world as rather restrictive and isolating in spite of the family reunion for the wedding. The presentation of Battle's, Troy's, and also of George's lives is confined to a depiction of more public affairs such as duties on the plantation (Battle), problems as overseer (Troy), or a quarrel with a wife (George). The prevailing female focalizers make the absence of the male voice even more noticeable. Lanser has observed the opposite tendency in Faulkner's *The Sound and the Fury* with regard to Caddie. In

Faulkner's novel Caddie has no voice at all, whereas the three Compson brothers alternately take the narrative role. In *Delta Wedding* the female focalization not only pushes the men and their voices into the background, but it contributes to the establishment of a matriarchal order. I no longer call it a "*grandly* matriarchal order" (my emphasis) as Prenshaw does because the focalizers' perceptions often reveal that they struggle with the role they have been given within this order. It is a matriarchal order ruling in the narrative realm. The predominant female point of view indeed brings forth an ideology that questions the sex-role system and even replaces the male-dominating structures with female ones—within the narrative realm.

# 3

# *The Golden Apples*: Female Myths and the Woman Artist

## MYTHOLOGICAL BACKGROUND

In 1955 Harry C. Morris considered *The Golden Apples* to be "experimental" because of Welty's use of mythology.[1] It is especially the fusion of ancient myths with the modern lives in the village of Morgana that strikes Morris as experimental. He lists three characteristics of Welty's use of Greek myths: her reliance on myth to impose some order on contemporary history, her creation of myths in modern life, which are then linked to their ancient forerunners, and finally her use of myths in order to control the structure and form of her work.[2] Morris mentions the myths of Danae and Perseus, parts of Zeus' and Aphrodite's encounters, and the wanderings of Odysseus, but he does not give a detailed analysis of the context in which these myths occur. I agree with his remark that Welty's *The Golden Apples* is indeed experimental, but not with his conclusion that it is "not always a successful experiment."[3] The reasons for the experimental vein do not only lie in the merging of ancient and modern myths, but in the particular mode of using different myths in connection with the female characters (e.g., Virgie, Cassie, or Miss Eckhart). Other critics have dwelt on Welty's use of mythology,[4] for example Danièle Pitavy-Souques, who, in a more recent article, uses a structural approach.[5] Like Morris, Pitavy-Souques observes that Welty incorporates myth according to T. S. Eliot's comment on Joyce's use of myth in *Ulysses*, namely that "it is simply a way of controlling, of ordering, of giving a shape and significance to the immense panorama of futility and anarchy which is contemporary history."[6] Pitavy-Souques emphasizes the myth of Perseus in connection with the themes and techniques of *The Golden Apples* and the way it appears in each chapter or story,[7] whereas Thomas McHaney investigates the allusions to numerous myths, both Celtic and Graeco-Roman. It is almost a characteristic of the criticism of *The Golden Apples* that the various myths are weighed differently. Each critic who deals with the myths selects different ones and concentrates on them.

Apart from Pitavy-Souques's focus on the Perseus myth her reference to the "repetition of the same stories,"[8] which are being reflected and quoted but at the same time created anew, is especially worth noting. Incidentally, it ties in with my initial remark about the rewriting process of myths (cf. my introduction). Pitavy also pays due attention to the aspect of intertextuality, which seems to be just as important in Welty's work as in Faulkner's.[9] In her impressive article on *The Golden Apples* and its connection with a poem by Yeats, Patricia Yaeger develops this aspect even further.[10] Making use of Bakhtin's thesis that language is "dynamic and plural" and that "it is populated—over-populated—with the intentions of others,"[11] she draws our attention to Welty's appropriation of "The Song of Wandering Aengus" and thus throws light on a female discourse contrasting the male-inscribed plot of the poem. The fragments of the poem that

Welty uses, "creat[e] a comparison between the half-articulated discourse of women's wishing and a well-defined male teleology."[12] Welty's references to Yeats's poem demonstrate that his images of the (male) wanderer are not rejected or simply transformed or "transsexed"[13] into her female characters; rather, besides questioning the male domain and sources of these images, they vividly reflect the specifically female way of reacting to them.[14]

Yaeger's insistence on the gender nature of Yeats's poem impels us to analyze it briefly. Moreover, the fact that Welty chose the last line from it for the title of her book must be considered. One of the female protagonists is continually reminded of a poem she had once come across in a book. Cassie Morrison's preoccupation with remembering the poem finally makes her sit up during her sleep and quote the line " 'Because a fire was in my head.' "[15] Yeats's poem has as its protagonist a male figure obsessed by a fire in his head. The fire evokes a desire in him to roam the woods, where he finds

> a glimmering girl
> with apple blossoms in her hair.[16]

After calling him by his name she vanishes, but he knows that he will find out her whereabouts, "[t]hough [he is] old with wandering." The speaker does not seem to be troubled by the girl's disappearance: the lapse of time till he finds her will be filled by his walks and wanderings. Very assertively he states that he will kiss her, walk with her and pluck

> The silver apples of the moon,
> The golden apples of the sun.

Patricia Yaeger aptly points out that the speaker stands for the poet, whose object in his search is the feminine muse. She enables the poet to fulfill his call for poetic creativity besides promising to gratify his desire for sensual pleasure.

Cassie Morrison, the woman in Welty's book, does not resemble the "glimmering girl" so much as she reminds us of the speaker's desire for fulfillment. What, then, is behind Welty's use of this male-gendered poem? By relying on images of male self-realization to express the quest of her female characters, Eudora Welty questions the exclusiveness of the relationship between the male creative spirit and the female passive muse. In the detailed analysis of the individual female characters I shall focus on the ways in which they represent the transformation from the male image of creativity to the image of a woman's desire and "fire."

An approach to Welty's use of Yeats's poem in terms of male images is even more pertinent if we consider the additional, though more indirect, references to another Yeats poem, "Leda and the Swan."[17] This famous poem also has a strong sexual and male-dominant tone. In Welty's story "Sir Rabbit," the third chapter of *The Golden Apples*, a young woman is raped by the Zeuslike King MacLain: "When she laid eyes on Mr. MacLain close, she staggered, he had such grandeur" (p. 95). In Yeats's poem Leda is "the staggering girl"[18] who is dropped by the rapist after the sexual assault.

Welty's recurring references to and transformations of Yeatsian stories and myths, as well as Greek mythology, lead us to the question whether we cannot assume that there is another logic behind them than the one of (male) Western civilization. This notion is expressed by Lévi-Strauss's statement that Western anthropologists have frequently overlooked or misunderstood the logic underlying myths of primitive tribes.[19] I am not arguing that Welty uses a non-Western logic in her way of dealing with and incorporating myths into her stories, but I wonder whether her approach to myths does not reflect a logic strongly determined and influenced by her sex. According to Lévi-Strauss's theory the message of a myth can be understood as long as a culture is homogeneous, even if there are new versions of a particular myth.[20] The homogeneity of a culture can no longer be guaranteed if we take into account a model of women's culture as it is outlined by the Ardeners or by Gerda Lerner.[21] Since women are subsumed under the dominant (male) structure but at the same time have a realm not occupied by men, we cannot speak of a homogeneous culture at all. Gender, therefore, can be responsible for a specific transformation of predominantly male myths.

In each of the stories that make up *The Golden Apples* different myths are referred to, and sometimes they are even mingled. Welty does not follow the line of a particular ancient work as, for example, Joyce does in his *Ulysses*, but there is a common theme that ties the stories together: man/woman as the "artist, or foreigner, or wanderer, all the same thing" (p. 180). The quotation from the chapter "Music from Spain" contains the wanderer already mentioned implicitly in the title *The Golden Apples* with the reference to Yeats's poem. The artist is related to more than one character, but with the exception of the Spanish guitar player[22] all of them are women. The foreigner is traditionally linked with the artist, and Miss Eckhart of our book is the most conspicuous example. Eudora Welty's theme of the wanderer, the artist, and the foreigner is as complex as it is in *Ulysses*, but it is much more decisively linked with the question of gender and its social implications.

## "SHOWER OF GOLD": KATIE RAINEY AS A FEMALE NARRATOR

Like a stage manager, Katie Rainey, an inhabitant of Morgana, introduces herself, giving the reader her name and first commenting on who has just passed by her. She addresses the reader in a confidential tone, especially since she informs us about the passer-by's husband King MacLain, who left his wife by walking out of their house one day. Katie's presentation of the relationship between Snowdie and King reveals that her sympathies are definitely with Snowdie, the deserted wife and mother, although she also seems fascinated by King.[23] Once again we are confronted with a woman's view of a woman's frequent fate. Yet, Snowdie MacLain's experience with her husband's disappearance is exceptional in certain ways: two years after his vanishing he orders his wife to meet him "in the woods" (p. 4). The outcome of this meeting are twins. Katie Rainey tells us that there are rumors going around about "children known and unknown, scattered-like" (p. 4) whom King MacLain is supposed to have fathered. The wandering King always comes back from his roamings and takes himself a woman. The implicit reference to Yeats's poem "Leda and the Swan" is not so obvious in this first chapter as it is in his encounter with Mattie Will in the chapter "Sir Rabbit." Yet the name "Snowdie" and her appearance—she is an albino—may refer to the poem, although the color white is of course associated with the swan, which is the seducer Zeus. Moreover, there is a literal reference to "swan": talking about King's decision to marry Snowdie, Katie Rainey uses the expression "I swan" (p. 4), which is a dialectal form of "I declare," or "I swear."[24] Of course, this reference to "swan" has nothing to do with the water bird, but the very use of this word emphasizes its importance. Snowdie's twins reflect a more direct parallel to the poem: Leda gave birth to twins after being raped by the swan. The mythological figure Danae (moon goddess), sometimes also identified with Leucothea (white goddess), whom Zeus visited in a shower of gold, is more likely to be linked with Snowdie. Katie describes Snowdie after she has informed her of her pregnancy: "It was like a shower of something had struck her, like she'd been caught out in something bright" (p. 6). Moreover, the title of this chapter, "Shower of Gold," implies a male assault on a woman imprisoned in a tower. The outcome of this assault is, on the mythological level, Perseus, the slayer of Medusa. This latter scene is depicted on a picture that deeply impresses Virgie Rainey, Katie's daughter, one of the most eminent female wanderers of the book.

Through the indirect references to Perseus and, ultimately, to Virgie, who yearns for a life different from and more "heroic" than her mother's, we are confronted in the first few pages of *The Golden Apples* with a range of allusions all tying in with the theme of the search for fulfillment (the golden apples) and the "heroic act" (p. 243; Perseus's deed).

Katie Rainey, the story-teller of the first chapter, apart from being the "messenger" of the mythological allusions, establishes an intimate relationship with the reader. She addresses him/her directly several times, using a colloquial style such as "So it went the way I told you" (p. 6), or "Don't ask me why" (p. 10). She introduces the reader to Snowdie and also to other characters of Morgana, focusing on Snowdie's experience with her husband, King. Katie as a female narrator and speaker renders Snowdie's encounter with King in such a confidential tone that one also thinks of a female addressee, because Katie's topic is a subject of gossip traditionally associated with female referents. Apart from the chapter "The Whole World Knows," we find in all the other stories of the book a more or less omniscient third-person narrator who at times enters the minds of the characters. The opening chapter with Virgie's mother as the observer and addresser starts with a report about a female inhabitant of Morgana. The last chapter of the book is mainly dedicated to the funeral of this very first narrator. At the funeral Katie's report is indirectly referred to again through Virgie Rainey's thought that "in a house of death . . . all the stories come evident, show forth from the person, become a part of the public domain. Not the dead's story, but the living's" (p. 210). One can say that Katie's first story has always been "public domain," but the other stories only "come evident" after her death—and at the end of the whole book.

*The Golden Apples* is not only a carefully structured book with respect to the myths mentioned above; the linkage between the single stories is also reflected in the narratological stance. The book opens with Katie's lively account of

Snowdie's relationship with King and ends with Katie's funeral: the first—and only—female first-person narrator is buried, and the book comes to its end with Virgie, the daughter of the dead narrator. Virgie takes over the function of the observer, but her voice, delivered through a third-person narrator, is somber and does not address the reader in her mother's direct and confidential tone.

Katie's important function as the first narrator in a book with several other narrators is also interesting with regard to Welty's transformation of the myths mentioned above. Her remarks on Snowdie, who is associated with Danae, reveal a close participation in Snowdie's life and fate. She is much more concerned about the experience of Snowdie than of King, who is associated with Zeus. Although she admits a certain fascination for King, she is deeply affected by Snowdie's life. Katie Rainey, whose surname suggests a relation with Danae's fate of being visited in a shower of gold, is the female narrator who tells her observations to a passer-by/the reader and not the Homeric bard.

## "JUNE RECITAL": THE TWO FEMALE WANDERERS, VIRGIE AND MISS ECKHART

The second story opens with a presentation of the deserted MacLain house. The reader is first acquainted with a male observer: Loch Morrison, a boy ill with malaria, watches the house through a telescope. In one room he perceives Virgie, now sixteen years old, together with a sailor. Loch, almost like a Peeping Tom, watches the two lovers chase each other and finally topple on a mattress to make love. The reader is not directly confronted with Loch's observations; a third-person narrator describes what the young boy can see through the telescope. Loch is too young to interpret the lovers' movements (e.g., they hold "their legs in an M," p. 26). In the chapter "Moon Lake" the sexual implications in connection with Loch are much more vividly present; Loch saves a girl from drowning and resuscitates her by lying on top of her body. But Loch does not seem to be aware of his sexuality. Moreover, in the chapter "June Recital" his attention is soon taken away from the lovers and is focused on an old woman in another room of the abandoned house trying to set it afire. It is Miss Eckhart, the former piano teacher of Morgana, who has taught Virgie, her favorite and most talented pupil.

Loch immediately realizes that the old woman is trying to burn the house down, because she carries old newspapers to the fireplace. He also senses "that something was being counted" (p. 23) in that house. But he is not aware of time, as is Miss Eckhart with the metronome she puts on the piano, the only piece of furniture in the room. When the woman starts to play a tune, the wheel of time turns back, and with it the point of view shifts to Cassie, Loch's sister and Virgie's friend.

Cassie recognizes the tune because Virgie used to play it during their piano lessons at Miss Eckhart's. The piece, "Fuer Elise," takes Cassie back to the time when Virgie refused to play with the ticking of the metronome, which Miss Eckhart finally accepted although she adored the little machine. Together with the tune "a line of poetry tumbled in her [Cassie's] ears" (p. 31); it is the line "Though I am old with wandering" from Yeats's poem. But Cassie is not like wandering Virgie; already as a girl she has felt that Virgie's future would be different from hers. Cassie as the still observer is contrasted with Virgie, who appears in Cassie's memories as the wild girl riding on a boy's bicycle. Cassie has always been in awe of Virgie's courage and of her gypsylike attitude, which made an inhabitant think that she "would be the first lady governor of Mississippi" (p. 38).

As Cassie continues to reminisce, a further striking capability of Virgie's is mentioned: she played "Fuer Elise" in such an exceptional way that a strange relationship developed between her and Miss Eckhart. Virgie found the "timid spot in her soul" (p. 40), Miss Eckhart's worshipping attitude towards her metronome. Virgie refused its beats, and thus set her own pace. Their awareness and sense of time tie them together. It is significant that in the last chapter, "The Wanderers," the narrator tells us that Virgie sees "things in their time," and therefore sees Perseus's beheading of Medusa in Miss Eckhart's picture "in three moments, not one" (p. 243).[25] In "June Recital" Miss Eckhart finally tries to stop time by burning down the house. The "fire in [Virgie's] head" is virtually catching Miss Eckhart's hair and head as she succeeds in lighting the house before she is taken away to an asylum.[26]

Both Virgie and Miss Eckhart are doomed to roam the world in their own ways: "Both . . . were human beings terribly at large, roaming on the face of the earth. And there were others of them—human beings, roaming, like lost beasts" (p. 85). These thoughts wander in Cassie's mind at night after she has watched the MacLain house catch fire and seen how Virgie, running out of the house, caught sight of Miss Eckhart for one moment. Full of impressions of this encounter Cassie all of a sudden remembers the entire Yeats poem. In her sleep she sits up and quotes the line "Because a fire was in my head." In her dreams a face appears to her: "the face that was in the poem" (p. 85). It is left open whether the face refers to "the glimmering girl" of the poem or to Miss Eckhart's "glimmering head." The face in the poem appears to Cassie after her vision of Virgie and Miss Eckhart, the female wanderers. Viewed within the context of Yeats's wandering Aengus we can say that they do not possess the self-assurance of Yeats's hero. An equivalent of "the glimmering girl" does not exist; there is no "glimmering boy" who would grant them a successful search.

Miss Eckhart, a German immigrant, has remained an outsider; the villagers do not accept her strange language and they do not understand what made her leave Europe for a southern village. Music could have been an equivalent of the "glimmering boy," but, as it turns out—as with many other single women at her time—teaching piano lessons to mostly untalented children does not make for fulfillment and self-realization. Her "last hope for vicarious fulfillment"[27] wanes, because Virgie does not heed her advice to get around in the world in order to improve her piano playing; instead, Virgie starts playing at the local café. Julia Mortimer, the teacher in *Losing Battles*, must also painfully accept that her pupil Gloria is not willing to teach school. Both Julia Mortimer and Miss Eckhart are examples of the single woman (teacher) who yearns for artistic or intellectual fulfillment but must recognize the limits of her aspirations.[28]

Miss Eckhart, whose "wanderings" have taken her furthest from her country, had her vision once while she played Beethoven, and Cassie, Virgie, and the other pupils were present; she played the music with such intensity that it "was too much for Cassie Morrison. It lay in the very heart of the stormy morning—there was something almost too violent about a storm in the morning" (p. 50). Miss Eckhart's passion for music is not only too much for Cassie; it is also too much for the people of Morgana. After she has been raped, they all wish she would move away. But she stays on and endures her lonely life as an outsider, as the wanderer who has not found her destination, neither locally nor emotionally. Virgie's experience also characterizes her as the outsider, but she finally has an epiphany that prevents her from committing such a desperate act as Miss Eckhart (cf. "The Wanderers").

The two wanderers, Virgie and Miss Eckhart, are each presented to us by a male and a female observer, Loch and Cassie, who focus on different aspects of the two. Loch with his telescope describes exterior traits of the two without realizing the tragic dimensions of the events in the MacLain house. He is interested in the action, welcoming the distraction while being confined to his room with malaria. Cassie, on the other hand, whose attention is caught because of the familiar tune she hears, is only an indirect observer because she does not see what is going on in the house. Yet her view of the two wanderers is much more informative and direct;

her memories encompass their characteristic traits in a more precise way than Loch, who uses his telescope with a clear lens. But through Cassie's "lenses" the two women are envisaged in a way that touches upon their respective tragedy with regard to their longings for fulfillment. Although Cassie cannot explain the reasons for the tragic impact, her remembrances refer to those aspects that are essential for the lives of the two women. Her observations from her room without direct view to the house show that from a woman's room—often associated with confinement and passivity—a broad and illuminating perspective is possible. Loch's direct gaze enables the reader to catch a glimpse of the two women, but his sister's point of view is necessary to make the reader aware of the "fire in [their] heads."[29] It is significant that Loch runs after the metronome, which a villager has taken from Miss Eckhart, although he cannot comprehend its meaning for Miss Eckhart and Virgie. He returns to his room with the telescope and the metronome, two technical devices, which allow a precise "measuring" of space and time. And yet his sister's comprehension of space and time with regard to the female wanderers is the more precise orientation for the reader. Loch's point of view together with the omniscient third-person narrator's is extended and given significance by Cassie's memories and her Cassandralike knowledge of the happenings.

## "SIR RABBIT" AND "LEDA AND THE SWAN"

In the third chapter King MacLain chases Mattie Will, who roams the woods together with her husband. King fires after him and he passes out. King "stood with head cocked . . . and then [Mattie Will] was caught by the hair and brought down as suddenly to earth as if whacked by an unseen shillelagh"[30] (pp. 94–95). The description of the rape is strikingly reminiscent of Yeats's language in the poem "Leda and the Swan." Welty even retains some of the wording and alliteration one finds in Yeats's poem ("she staggered, he had such grandeur, and then she was caught" or "Then when he let her fall and walked off, when he was out of hearing in the woods and the birds and wood-sounds and the wood-chopping throbbed clearly," p. 95). Welty's language is as poetic as Yeats's, and one can indeed attribute Geoffrey Hartman's words to hers when he talks about "Leda and the Swan":

> Mimesis becomes poesis, imitation becomes making, by giving form and pressure to a presumed reality, to "Leda." The traditional theme, by being repeated, is endowed with a past that may never have been present.[31]

However, Welty's use of "the traditional theme" is not only repeated; it is also extended, for the story goes on for the victim of the rape; the narrator describes how and what Mattie Will feels after having been dropped like an object. Patricia Yaeger speaks of a revision of Yeats's poem in the sense that Welty is interested in Mattie Will's wanderings and not in the rapist's.[32] The point of view is with Mattie, who walks in the woods where "she heard sounds, the dry creek beginning to run or a strange man calling" (p. 96). She finally comes across King MacLain again, who is asleep under a tree, snoring. She watches him with care, glad that she now is free to look at him. The narrator describes "the King" with a tinge of irony: his body appears to her like "her man's now, or of any more use than a heap of cane thrown up by the mill and left in the pit to dry" (pp. 96–97). After his assault the aggressor is exposed to the victim without his knowing. Yet, Mattie Will does not forget the sexual attack; it even makes her recall her experience with King MacLain's twins, who once attacked her in the wood and sat on her with "their little aching Adam's apples" (p. 98).

Strangely enough, Mattie is also fascinated by King and

even seems to enjoy his aggressive love-making. Unlike "Leda" in Yeats's poem, who "is but the legendary medium,"[33] she is presented as the one who roams the woods and seeks an adventure. The sexual dimension with regard to Mattie Will, who is a victim of the males' "will," refers to the Yeats poem, but it also refers to a new text whose protagonist is female and thus incorporates a woman who is no longer only "the glimmering girl" as the object for the wandering Aengus.

## "MOON LAKE": RAPE AND REBIRTH

In her article on "Moon Lake," Patricia Yaeger focuses on Welty's use of phallic imagery and poses the question: how should we respond to it when we come across it in a woman's text, since the phallus, according to Lacan, marks the texts of male writers and of patriarchal culture in general?[34] If a woman's text teems with phallic images we might expect a "displacement,"[35] which has effects on the traditional patterns of sex roles.

Loch Morrison, with his name denoting "lake" in Irish, is the hero of "Moon Lake." As we know from "June Recital," he cannot play music, but he can save lives. "Loch Morrison, Boy Scout and Life Saver" (p. 99), as he is called at the outset of the chapter, spends a week in a girls' camp at the lake. He is the quiet observer, he hardly speaks with the girls, and he only swims in the lake when none of the girls are in it. The difference between the descriptions of the girls and Loch swimming in the lake is an illustrative example of the difference between the sexes: the male swimmer dives, goes "through the air rocking and jerking like an engine, splashed in, climbed out, spat, climbed up again" (p. 100), whereas the female swimmers "stood waistdeep and waited for the dip to be over" (p. 102); "they swam and held to the rope, hungry and waiting" (p. 103). The descriptions contain the traditional separation between the active, aggressive, and physically stronger male, and the careful, anxious, and physically feeble female. The imagery used in describing the girls' immersion in the water is often phallic:

> If they let their feet go down, the invisible bottom of the lake felt like knee-deep fur. The sharp hard knobs came up where they were least expected. The Morgana girls of course wore bathing slippers, and the mud loved to suck them off. (p. 103)

The phallic symbols not only emphasize the male-dominated world of the girls, they are also intensifiers for Loch's masculine presence. Every morning he wakes the girls with his bugle, the shape of which already suggests the phallus: "He blew his horn into their presence—trees' and girls'—and then watched the Dip [into the water]" (p. 100). Loch's horn controls the girls' sleep, and it is not surprising that he can also control lives, that is, girls' lives.

The incident of the resuscitation of an orphaned girl called Easter is the climax of the increasingly aggressive masculine imagery. Loch's attempt to save Easter's life strongly resembles a rape. The very beginning of the rescue operation bears traits of rape imagery. The girls "saw him snatch the hair of Easter's head, the way a boy will snatch anything he wants, as if he won't have invisible opponents snatching first" (p. 126). The general judgment about the recklessness of boys who want to reach their goal without having to fear (female) opposition intensifies the sexual implication of the rape of a helpless girl.

The description of Easter, who is put on a table, contrasts with that of the "snatching" boy. The narrator also refers to the sexual realm of Easter's gender, but in a different way. Easter's body seems to be calm, soft, yet exposed to an attack or willed assault: "She was arm to arm and leg to leg in a long fold, wrong-colored and pressed together as unopen leaves are. Her breasts, too, faced together" (p. 128). Since we know that Easter has already "started her breasts" (p. 105) and that in her eyes "there might have been women's heads, ancient" (p. 106), her almost mythical femaleness is laid bare before Loch, the male life-saving hero.

When he starts to work on Easter, "goug[ing] out her mouth with his hand" (p. 128), the narrator herself explicitly expresses astonishment ("an unbelievable act," p. 128) and comments on the other girls' reaction, implying horror and fear: "Life-saving was much worse than they had dreamed. Worse still was the carelessness of Easter's body" (p. 129). Even without these comments, the life-saving act bears traits of a violent attack against the girl: "with a groan of his own [he] fell upon her and drove up and down upon her, into her, gouging the heels of his hands into her ribs again and again" (p. 129). This rape imagery occurs several times in the course of the resuscitation, and it becomes sexually more direct the more closely Loch comes to bringing Easter back to life. The climax of the seemingly sexual union ("the Boy-Scout seemed for ever part of Easter and she part of him," p. 133) almost coincides with Easter's gaining consciousness. Thus, the climax to the rape is at the same time the moment of rebirth. As her name suggests, Easter returns to the living like Christ; Loch, like God the Father, is the "reviver," though not of His son but of an orphan girl. Thus, a reversal of the (male) Christian tradition is implied.[36] Easter herself even writes her name in the sand as "Esther," an act that on the one hand demonstrates that she can name herself, and on the other refers to a female Biblical hero.

Some critics have pointed out that Easter is metaphorically raped, but others have altogether dismissed such a thought or reference. Louis Rubin even feels that Loch's heroic act is not approved of by the community, and that "his companions feel awkward at his action."[37] Yet, I think it is due to Welty's narrative strategy that the "heroic" act undergoes a transformation. Loch's life-saving act loses its character of rescue because it is viewed by females only and is presented as an act of violation. The heroic act is being stripped of its heroism. It becomes an act of violation against the female, and thus must be seriously questioned. Moreover, the victim—or saved girl—kicks her "deliverer" as soon as she has gained consciousness. The values of the heroic act are no longer linked with the exclusively male domain. Therefore, it is not surprising that it is Virgie, the woman, who recognizes the true heroic act (cf. chapter on "The Wanderers").

The "displacement" of the phallus mentioned above is referred to at the end of "Moon Lake" in a striking and even comic way: the two girls Nina and Jinny Love watch Loch Morrison undress in his tent. The narrator's ironic comment now undermines Loch's accomplishment of the day; the irony is even mirrored in the use of her vocabulary: "He was naked and there was his little tickling thing hung on him like the last drop on the pitcher's lip" (p. 137). The hero of the day, who saved Easter with his masculine attitude of attack, appears to the reader, and to the two girls, like a little boy with diminished genitals with no power at all; on the contrary, the "little tickling thing" is a ridiculous attribute that makes the two girls and the (female?) reader feel superior, and they recognize the conceit of "his silly, brief, overriding little show" (p. 138). As in "Sir Rabbit," after King has raped Mattie Will, the male is unmasked when exposed to the female observer without his knowledge: "the dangling signifier"[38] no longer denotes male potency and dominance. We are reminded of Annie Leclerc's suggestion to "simply deflate his [man's] values with the needle of ridicule."[39]

Rape is a theme Welty employs in order to demonstrate the fate of the female, but it is also a means to make the female recognize the difference "between the raper's value of her only as a sexual object and her own sense of self-worth as a woman seeking love."[40] In her short story "At the Landing," Welty presents the female protagonist as the wanderer who can set out on her journey after the terrible experience of being raped. The protagonist must choose between captivity or rape, and she chooses the latter of the two dismal alternatives. As in "Moon Lake," rape is closely linked with rebirth; the insight that has been gained at the cost of a terrible experience illustrates that the female must pay a price connected with her gender. Although both Easter and Jenny are victims of men's power, they refuse to die, both symbolically and factually. Especially in the case of Jenny, the future outlined in the story suggests a life, which allows her more self-responsibility and autonomy.[41]

The various references to the questionable attitude of the male "hero" in "Moon Lake" reveal that after the act the phallus is no longer a powerful instrument. It is not surprising that the two girls, at the sight of Loch Morrison with his "Minnowy thing" (p. 138), declare that they "always want to be old maids" (p. 138). After the illustration of male power in the girls' camp the girls are able to unmask this phallic power as "Minnowy." This recognition weakens the male image of the phallus designating power and creativity and transforms it to the "little tickling thing," which can hardly stand for power. Patriarchal power is still reality when we think of the various rapes taking place in *The Golden Apples*, but it has lost its dominating force for the female. The myth of the male hero and wanderer with his urge for creativity and power is being taken over by the female, whose desire is not yet very concrete, but nevertheless real; the "fire in [her] head" is burning. The fire in the woman's head also weakens the power of the phallus; the female urge to persevere (in death and rebirth) makes the male's momentary "creative" outburst look diminished in comparison.

In terms of the (transformed) myths, Loch bears resemblance to Perseus, who saved the naked girl Andromeda from a sea monster, but unlike Perseus, Loch and the saved girl are not united. On the contrary, Loch remains in his tent by himself without triumph and trophy.

## "THE WHOLE WORLD KNOWS": A MAN'S FEARS

"The Whole World Knows" is the only story told by a first-person male narrator. King MacLain's son Randall tells us about his frustrated life as a husband who has been deserted by his wife. In the very first sentence he addresses his father, admitting how much he wishes to talk to him about his predicament. This introductory statement sounds as if the following "I" narration were an attempt to communicate with a father who is still present. The communicative act is essential for Ran to articulate his hurt feelings. The reader can expect a confidential report because he/she has to take the role of Ran's father as an addressee. In the course of his monologue Ran addresses his father—and at times also his mother—when his distress seems worst, yet it is the reader who must listen. Indeed, "the whole world must know," because Ran has nobody he could confide in.

"The Whole World Knows" is also a chapter about sex and power between the sexes; Michael Kreyling adequately states that in this chapter "sex has become a battleground."[42] Ran, who is enraged by Jinny's infidelity, is obsessed with wreaking revenge on women, and he therefore takes Maideen Sumrall, a young woman from Morgana, to a motel room. He frightens her to death by aiming a pistol at her first, before putting it into his mouth and pulling the trigger, but the pistol does not fire. Maideen takes the pistol from him, and Ran makes love to her. It is finally Maideen who kills herself shortly after her horrifying encounter with Ran. Indirectly, Ran has killed her all the same, because, as it later turns out, she has taken this affair very seriously. Ran, on the other hand, has tried to kill in his fantasy before: his fantasized killing of his wife Jinny bears signs of his grudge against the opposite sex:

> I saw her pouting childish breasts, excuses for breasts, sprung full of bright holes where my bullets had gone.

> But Jinny didn't feel it. She threaded her needle. She made her little face of success. Her thread always went straight in the eye. (pp. 151–152)

In the fight between Ran and Jinny the woman is the winner; already in "Moon Lake" she was a girl of self-assertion and fearlessness. Ran, who has attacked Mattie Will together with his twin brother Eugene (cf. "Sir Rabbit"), is now the loser in this "thing of the flesh" (p. 146), as a gossiping Morgana woman describes Ran's marriage problems. Everybody, that is, "the whole world," will know about his failure; Morgana is "the whole world" for him; and he cannot get away like his father King MacLain or his brother Eugene. Ran is defeated now, although he will later be the winner in the mayoral election of Morgana. But in the war between the sexes he, a victim himself, has left a female victim behind. Maideen Sumrall, because of her suicide, is figuratively shot in her breasts by Ran, even though he had fantasized about shooting Jinny.

At the end of his monologue Ran addresses his father and brother directly. He asks them whether they have found something better than Ran when they went out into the world. The answer to this question is never given, and it is again through Virgie in the last chapter that we shall recognize the genuine and well-understood quest of the wanderer in *The Golden Apples.*

Compared to the other stories "The Whole World Knows" does not teem with references to myth. Thomas McHaney mentions Yeats's "No Second Troy," in which Yeats complains that modern men no longer have the courage "equal to desire"[43] Greek warriors demonstrated. Ran, the modern man, restlessly drives through the streets of Morgana till he picks up Maideen, but, as we know, he cannot win back Jinny.[44] Looking at Yeats's poem more closely, one detects that Welty's story contains another allusion to the poem: like the speaker of the poem, Ran asks questions in connection with his beloved woman; furthermore, he blames Maideen for having "hurt herself" (p. 160). But unlike Yeats's speaker, who at the end of the poem releases the girl (Maud Gonne) from her guilt by blaming her "Troy-less"[45] age, Ran is caught up in his aggressive feelings towards the opposite sex. His view of Jinny does not convey the idea of the legendary Helen at all. Instead, in his monologue, he puts all the blame on the others, while he presents himself as the victim. Indeed, he appears to the reader as a self-pitying, narrow-minded person who "stays in Morgana and grows fat."[46] He is definitely no wanderer with an honorable quest in mind.

## "MUSIC FROM SPAIN:" THE ULYSSEAN WANDERER

After Ran's "story" we are confronted with that of his twin brother Eugene, which is told by a third-person narrator; various passages are written in the mode of the indirect interior monologue. Eugene is married to a notoriously malcontented woman with whom he had a daughter who had died. One morning Eugene slaps his wife without any obvious reason,[47] and leaves her in a haunted state of mind. He roams the city of San Francisco aimlessly. He catches sight of a Spaniard who played the guitar in a concert Eugene and his wife attended the previous evening. Eugene saves his life when he unexpectedly walks in front of an approaching car. The two men shake hands and continue their way together through town without being able to speak the other's language. Reminiscent of Bloom's roaming in "The Lotus Eaters,"[48] the two wander through the streets, moving together in time and space. The Spaniard is the representative of the wandering artist with his instrument on his back, but he cannot communicate his experiences to Eugene. Nevertheless, Eugene feels attracted to him. He seems to him "the perfect being to catch up with," "a stranger and yet not a stranger" (p. 171). Eugene is eager to stay together with this stranger because he finally senses "a secret in the day" (p. 174). The narrator puts his desire for "the secret" in a more general context: she includes the reader in her question, which alludes to the title of her book once again, "Was it so strange, the way things are flung out at us, like the apples of Atalanta perhaps, once we have begun a certain onrush?" (p. 174).

The allusion to the Greek myth of the apples of Atalanta has yet a slightly different connotation from that of the Yeats poem with its male searcher. In the Atalanta myth it is the woman who is the huntress, and she has been able to intrude into the band of the bravest hunters of Greece. Atalanta, the virgin huntress, wanted to remain single, but finally had to yield to her father's wish that she should marry. Melanion defeated her in the foot race, which every suitor had to run with her, by throwing three golden apples into her path. Atalanta could not resist stopping and picking them up, and thus lost the race. The golden apples representing a negative distraction for Atalanta bear a positive connotation in the narrator's question, because Eugene is unexpectedly confronted with the Spaniard, who embodies the unknown, "the secret." Furthermore, Eugene's "distraction" enables him to leave his ordinary life behind him for one day.

By referring to the apples of Atalanta, Welty again makes use of a classical myth in an altered form. In a chapter dedicated to a male wanderer she mentions the Atalanta myth with its female protagonist, whereas in the chapters dealing with female wanderers she relies on myths with predominantly male protagonists. It seems as if Welty deliberately wanted to reverse the gender roles. The references to the Yeats poem with its Celtic (and Greek) mythological background mainly occur with regard to females (Cassie, Virgie, Miss Eckhart). Of course, in "Music from Spain" there are other mythological allusions together with the explicit mentioning of Atalanta. The Perseus story is especially pertinent to the relationship between Eugene and the Spaniard; Thomas McHaney has even stated that Eugene "replays the Perseus story,"[49] and that like Perseus, Eugene wanders to the very west ("Land's End," p. 191) where he will have a fight with an opponent who excels him in size and strength. But unlike Perseus, who can use the Gorgon's head in order to outwit Atlas, Eugene has no trophy that could assist him in his fight against the giant. It is the Spaniard who, after Eugene's assault, throws Eugene up into the air at the edge of the cliff as if Eugene were a child. This incident is not only threatening to Eugene; he also feels "greatest comfort" while being lifted up: "He was without a burden in the world" (p. 197). Ruth M. Vande Kieft states that Eugene experiences a kind of rebirth in those strong hands of the Spanish artist.[50] Eugene's relationship with the Spaniard strongly suggests that Eugene is also attracted to the latter because he feels safe and sound like a child who finds comfort with his mother. The Spaniard is described as having female traits: his fingernails are painted in a bright red (cf. p. 173), his hair hangs "behind him almost to his shoulders" (p. 172), and when he once catches his hat to prevent it from flying away in the wind, his elbows are bent and he takes "the lumpy pose of a woman, a 'nude reclining' " (p. 193). It is no coincidence that Eugene thinks of his wife Emma exactly at the very moment when he feels at ease in the Spaniard's presence, both physically and emotionally. His thoughts about his wife concern his return to their house, which, he knows, is inevitable; being lifted up in the air again by his companion, Eugene has a vision of a sexual encounter between himself and Emma. In this vision it is not the man who is sexually aggressive, but Emma, who forces herself upon her husband. Eugene, in his place, seems to be sexually aroused by the Spaniard: he "was upborne, open-armed. He was only thinking, My dear love comes" (p. 198). It seems as if Eugene's desire for "a secret in the day" is inextricably intertwined with love. This love is not the traditionally sanctified love between a man and a woman, but the love, or attraction, between a man looking for fulfillment and another man representing love, art (music), and exoticism for the former:

> Eugene clung to the Spaniard now, almost as if he had waited for him a long time with longing, almost as if he loved him, and had found a lasting refuge. He could have caressed the side of the massive face with the great pores in the loose, hanging cheek. (p. 195)

"Music from Spain" is the only story in which a relationship between two men is described, and it is no coincidence that the descriptions of both men have female characteristics. In fact, Welty never depicts relationships entirely bound to tradition as far as gender roles are concerned, and even in "Moon Lake," where the traditional roles seem to be granted (Loch, the male life saver; the girls, the female hesitant "nonswimmers"), Welty questions these roles by unmasking certain characteristics of the division between the sexes. In "Music from Spain" the unusual description of the Spaniard and the attraction he represents for Eugene lessen the impact of the male heroic attitude.

Although Eugene experiences a moment of intense and serene satisfaction in the presence of the Spaniard, he knows well that they must part. The inevitable separation takes place in a noncommittal atmosphere. After having coffee together in a cafe they "turned to each other almost formally" (p. 201), and Eugene runs for the next streetcar, which brings him back to his everyday life with Emma. In the last chapter, "The Wanderers," we learn that he returns to Morgana, but without his wife. He dies of tuberculosis at quite an early age. McHaney aptly states that "like Miss Eckhart and Mrs. Morrison and other dissatisfied wanderers and sojourners, he is buried near Morgana."[51] Eugene's yearning for "the secret of the day" has been fulfilled for one day only; he has not been able to become the artistlike figure he admires in the Spaniard.

"Music from Spain," the section before the final story, "The Wanderers," has a protagonist who shares characteristics with Perseus, the archetypal wanderer, but it must be pointed out that he is not successful in his search at all. As mentioned before, the female protagonist of the last story, Virgie, comes closest to the wanderer in whom characteristics of the foreigner and the artist are united.

## "THE WANDERERS": VIRGIE AND HER WANDERING DREAMS

In the last story of *The Golden Apples*, Katie Rainey, the narrator of the first story, has just died, and people in Morgana are busy preparing for the funeral. Their ritual attendance at the funeral emphasizes the fact that, figuratively speaking, the description of Morgana and its inhabitants is approaching its conclusion. We know that those inhabitants who have been wanderers have not really succeeded in their search. Virgie Rainey, the dead woman's daughter, is the protagonist of the last story, and she is the embodiment of the wanderer who does not seem to be defeated.

Virgie is now over forty years old, and she is still a rebellious woman in that she does not conform to the notions the others have of a woman at her age. She lives an independent life, as she did when she was a girl, although she has looked after her old mother most dutifully before she died. In "June Recital" Virgie appears to us as a very sensuous young woman, and at forty she is still described as being a vigorous woman, who has a very strong bodily presence apart from her spiritual longings and abilities. Now, on the evening before her mother's funeral, Virgie goes swimming in the Big Black River. Naked, she "hung suspended in the Big Black River as she would know to hang suspended in felicity" (p. 219). The various descriptions of her experience in the river suggest a harmony between Virgie's body and the surroundings of nature. The unity between her and the water, the shells, the sand, the grass, and the mud is like a sexual union, and the following passage even refers to bodily movements during the sexual act:

> She felt the sand, grains intricate as little cogged wheels, minute shells of old seas, and the many dark ribbons

> of grass and mud touch her and leave her, like suggestions and withdrawals of some bondage that might have been dear, now dismembering and losing itself. (p. 219)

The sexual imagery suggests that Virgie experiences nature's closeness as a "bondage," but at the same time the "dismembering" implies a separation typical of Virgie's independence and attempt to break bonds that might hold her. Floating in the river, Virgie feels free and "suspended," and we are reminded of an earlier description of a woman swimming in the water and experiencing absolute freedom: in Kate Chopin's *The Awakening* the protagonist Edna Pontellier swims out in the sea, naked and by herself, and she, too, is encircled by the water in a "soft, close embrace."[52] The nature imagery also implies that the woman experiences freedom for herself although she is one with nature.

The sexual suggestion in the description of literary female landscapes is a feature frequently occurring in writings by women. The various references to the sensations of female characters while swimming in the sea or in a river often point to "oceanic feelings"[53] traditionally experienced by men going to the sea. It is no coincidence that women writers frequently describe women characters swimming or bathing in a river or the sea, some of them, like Virgie or Edna Pontellier, naked and experiencing total freedom. Ellen Moers points out that many of the female landscapes express "emotions ranging from the erotic to the mystical."[54] Welty's description of Virgie's bath in the Big Black River[55] can be placed somewhere in the middle of this spectrum. It is both erotic and mystical: the erotic aspect, having nothing to do with a male person, concerns Virgie alone, whereas the mystical aspect is present in the regenerating dimension of the bath. The nature descriptions refer to female freedom in a sense that encompasses both spiritual and bodily independence. Virgie's experience in the river gives her new strength for future wanderings and roamings, although she must first face her mother's funeral. The Big *Black* River is not only a symbol of eros and rebirth, it is also associated with death; the river as a symbol contains Eros and Thanatos, love and death, close together.

The last chapter deals with death, and yet it bears traits of rebirth and regeneration. For Virgie, the wanderer, it is significant that death and rebirth are so close together. The narrator makes it quite clear that Virgie has this knowledge: she "never doubted that all the opposites on earth were close together, love close to hate, living to dying; but of them all, hope and despair were the closest blood" (p. 234). Virgie's insight into the forces of life make her unique among all the other inhabitants of Morgana, even among those who are wanderers like her. The archetypal quality of her being a female wanderer is summarized towards the end of the book, and it is connected with female heroism:

> Cutting off the Medusa's head was the heroic act, perhaps, that made visible a horror in life, that was at once the horror in love, Virgie thought—the separateness. She might have seen heroism prophetically when she was young and afraid of Miss Eckhart. She might be able to see it now prophetically, but she was never a prophet. Because Virgie saw things in their time, like hearing them—and perhaps because she must believe in the Medusa equally with Perseus—she saw the stroke of the sword in three moments, not one. In the three was the damnation—no, only the secret, unhurting because not caring in itself—beyond the beauty and the sword's stroke and the terror lay their existence in time—far out and endless, a constellation which the heart could read over many a night. (p. 243)

The heroic act, which refers mainly to a male domain, is used in order to illustrate a woman's search for and understanding of herself and the universe. The mentioning of Miss Eckhart's picture with Perseus and Medusa's head at this moment of Virgie's epiphanylike recognition indicates a transformation of the male heroic act. Miss Eckhart used to compare this heroic act to Siegfried's slaying the dragon, another example of the male tradition of struggling against and defeating life-threatening forces. Virgie not only dares to face the dragon and its horrifying effect ("a horror in life"), she also recognizes the importance of fighting the monster(s) that might keep human beings, females above all, imprisoned and paralyzed within their "safer" surroundings. In their study on female heroes Pearson and Pope point out that "when she [the hero] slays the dragons, she becomes, or is united with, her true self."[56] Virgie does not undergo a heroic journey in order to slay the dragon or the monster, nor is her search presented "as a retreat into a state of contemporary madness; as an adventure in the world of dreams, fantasy, and science fiction."[57] Virgie's heroic act takes place mainly within herself, i.e., she first kills the dragons, within herself,[58] that might prevent her from leading an independent life and from "[g]oing away" (p. 231) again immediately after her mother's funeral. Virgie will undertake further wanderings, although she does not explicitly articulate the object of her search. It is reasonable to argue that it will not be "a glimmering girl" as in Yeats's poem. Virgie's quest does not have a definite goal dependent on another person; she embodies movement towards hope, towards the future. Michael Kreyling mentions her "right to the name Virgie—ever new, whole."[59]

Virgie's recognition and awareness of the forward movement is related to her concept of time. She sees "things in their time," and thus is able to "believe in the Medusa equally with Perseus." The heroic act of cutting off Medusa's head is not perceived as an isolated deed, but as one that also has a victim, namely the Medusa. In her early study on Eudora Welty, Ruth M. Vande Kieft refers to this dual quality by pointing out that victims are necessary to the heroic act.[60] For Vande Kieft Virgie is a human being and not a hero; she can witness the heroic act, but she cannot experience it herself. Yet I think that Virgie's ability to grasp the tragic dualism of the heroic act also makes her "heroic." Medusa viewed as a victim is especially significant when we think of the implied myth that men were turned into stone if they looked at her. Freud's interpretation of the myth refers to castration anxiety and to Medusa's head as the castrated state of female genitals.[61] Virgie now realizes that the heroism of cutting off Medusa's head contains destruction with both its horror and its triumph, and she therefore emphasizes her belief in the Medusa. As in May Sarton's poem "The Muse as Medusa," where the suppressed (female) speaker recognizes herself in the face of the Medusa and thanks her for the "frozen rage" she sees,[62] Medusa is not only presented as a negative figure turning men to stone, but also as a victim on whom power is exercised.

Welty's emphasis on the Perseus myth in connection with Virgie has a specific function among all the other various references to myths: it not only encompasses the hero and his deed but also includes the victim, who is a female figure, even though a Gorgon.[63] The heroic act is understood by Virgie with its positive and negative implications; "the opposites on earth," which Virgie recognizes, are also true for the hero. Remembering Miss Eckhart at this point, Virgie significantly discovers that Miss Eckhart "had absorbed the hero and the victim" (p. 243), a fact that made her play Beethoven with all her abilities as an artist. The endless repetition of Perseus's striking off Medusa's head (cf. p. 243) refers to an equally repetitive form of heroic deed, the heroic creation.[64] The artist must forever recreate experiences without the assurance of their outcome. Yeats's Aengus appears to us self-assured, even though the "glimmering girl" vanishes. Virgie, as the embodiment of the female wanderer and artist, recognizes the necessity of repetition and the ever-beginning search of the artist for creativity.

The Medusa myth with its Freudian connotation of the feared female genitals also appears in Iris Murdoch's *A Severed Head*, in which a strange woman speaks of herself as "a severed head"[65] and tells a man about the "strange knowledge" he might acquire through her.[66] Robert Scholes mentions this central image in Murdoch's novel, stating that "the severed head represents literature itself, which, unlike philosophy, speaks mantically like an oracle."[67] Scholes comments on the Medusa myth in connection with the relationship of structuralism to existentialism, concluding that Murdoch's use of the severed head "is figuring her own leap from Sartrean freedom to Lévi-Straussean order, from contingency to pattern, from existentialism to structuralism."[68] He argues that Murdoch's characters are not alienated from each other but always related to each other, thus, having love as their principle. Sexual differentiation, he says, is the basis of all our being and thinking. Like Barbara Johnson, who maintains that literature is "also an incorrigible perpetrator of the problem of sexuality,"[69] Scholes believes in the essential influence of sexual difference, which is especially pertinent to a writer's vision. He attributes to existentialism a male view, whereas structuralism is dependent on female perception. Referring to Fowles's *The French Lieutenant's Woman*, he claims that "men see things and women see the relationships between things." Therefore, "the artist is likely to be himself an Eve-man or herself an Adam-woman."[70] Virgie Rainey, who recognizes the "three moments" and both the slayer and the victim, that is, the relationship between them, is also a representative of this kind of artist.

The Perseus myth and the Aengus myth are combined in Virgie's vision of the universe, the former being perceived as the ambivalent heroic act with its hero and victim, the latter as a possibility of translating the male heroic search for the muse into a female wandering. Virgie's ability to grasp both Perseus and Medusa separately is dependent on her concept of time. As mentioned above, Virgie sees Perseus's act in three moments, which can be interpreted as the past, the present, and the future. Time is essential in Welty's work, and it is also pertinent to its southern background: it is a southern characteristic to be aware of the past as well as of the future and the immediate present.[71] But this analysis has shown that Virgie is not only a typical representative of southern history, but first and foremost a representative of a female wanderer. Her desire is not quenched in the course of the story Welty describes; on the contrary, her longings are exemplary of a woman who will proceed with her search for "the golden apples," and whose fire will keep on burning without "a glimmering girl" in the background. Her wanderings are very much like the heroic journey of the archetypal hero, although they are not aimed at a particular goal.[72] Virgie's desire and seeking are essential, not the outcome of the search.

Virgie, then, is the only one of the Morgana wanderers who is not disillusioned or defeated. Her aspiration to "always wish[ing] for a little more of what had just been" (p. 220) will make her go on future wanderings. She is the extraordinary female wanderer who will not only be a foreigner again, but also a kind of artist. The image of the artist implied in the Yeats poem seems to be pertinent to Virgie, the woman, and not to any other (male) characters of the whole book; like an artist, she remains whole and autonomous,[73] and she has the last word of the whole book as the daughter of Katie Rainey, who started the book.

The last words of the book once again refer to the ancient myths, which are still omnipresent: "the running of the horse and bear, the stroke of the leopard, the dragon's crusty slither, and the glimmer and the trumpet of the swan" (p. 244). They mostly refer to heroic deeds achieved by males (Perseus, Hercules), and it is therefore all the more significant that it is Virgie and an old black beggar woman[74] who hear these mythical animals. Virgie, accompanied by the old woman called Minerva (goddess of wisdom), accepts her loneliness and is therefore wiser and freer than all the other characters of Morgana. She is the woman artist who has perhaps only created the story, which comes to its end when the first narrator—Katie Rainey—has died. The daughter keeps on wandering—creating new stories, perhaps. Like

Circe in the short story of the same name, the female protagonist remains by herself, but the text created anew by the dominance of the female is liberated (cf. my introduction, pp. 10–11).

# 4

# *Losing Battles*: Talking, Hiding, and Revealing, or Community and the Female Outsiders

## THE SPEECH ACT IN *LOSING BATTLES*

It is not surprising that *Losing Battles* is the least-discussed novel in Welty criticism. The form of the novel consists of dramatic techniques belonging more to the traditional epic[1] than to the modern novel: most of this rather lengthy book is written in direct dialogue, and the characters seem to talk together almost constantly. The difficulty of reviewers and critics in attributing the book to a particular genre[2] gives further evidence of its complex form.

The topic of the book is the family: one of the critics, Robert Heilman, even mentions the work together with other family dramas such as Eliot's *Family Reunion* or Albee's *The American Dream*.[3] Most of the members of the Renfro, Beecham, and Vaughn families that come together to celebrate Granny Vaughn's ninetieth birthday are presented through speech, and, as Welty herself has stated, "without benefit of the author's telling any more about what was going on inside the characters' minds and hearts."[4] Thus, Welty's narration is characterized by showing and not by telling, and the speeches are speech acts in the linguistic sense of the word. Welty, probably without having in mind the modern speech act theory, speaks of "translating every thought and feeling into action and speech, speech being another form of action."[5] The more traditional mode of narration through showing is obviously intended to "make everything shown, brought forth."[6] The frequently unmediated dialogue does not provide the reader with any information as to how he/she has to understand the characters' utterances. Seymour Chatman stresses the fact that in novels or stories predominantly composed of dialogues,

> to a greater degree than normal, the reader is required to interpret the illocutionary force of the sentences that are spoken by the characters; that is, he is supposed to infer what they 'mean' in the context of the action, even if there are no direct reports of that action, indeed even if the whole action can only be constructed through such inferences.[7]

The presentation of the characters' speeches without mediation in the form of the so-called "direct tagged speech"[8] does not, or does very rarely, allow the narrator, who is present all the same, to give comments or interpret the speeches. Mediation begins when the tags consist of verbs such as "to warn," "to insinuate," and "to command." In *Losing Battles* Welty employs such verbs, but "she said" and "he said," used numerously, force the reader to make the necessary inferences mentioned above.

Eudora Welty's comment on her use of speech records reveals that she attempted to get away from "description, . . . introspection on the part of [her] characters."[9] In her previous novels and in many of her stories she penetrates into the minds of her characters, and we have seen that she concentrates especially on the thoughts and feelings of her female characters (cf. *Delta Wedding*). In her essays on writers and writing Welty often mentions the interior of characters, that which "lies beneath the surface," or "that which is true under the skin, that which will remain a fact of the spirit."[10] The narrative mode for the exploration of the interior realm in conventional fiction seldom occurs in the transcription of direct speech as it appears in *Losing Battles*. Welty is aware of the difficult task with which a writer is confronted when he/she wants to present a character's thoughts, feelings, and reactions to his/her social environment and yet wishes to rely merely on speech report:

> Sometimes I needed to make a speech do three or four or five things at once—reveal what the character said but also what he thought he said, what he hid, what others were going to think he meant, and what they understood, and so forth—all in his single speech.[11]

Her statement on the writer's difficulties with pure dialogue also holds true for the reader, as Chatman points out. The reasons for the reader's difficulties in inferring meaning derive from the necessity to judge and to interpret texts according to our knowledge of the society we live in. If we come across speech acts with no additional references as to how to read them, we must entirely rely upon our own cultural and societal background, which can enhance the difficulty of reading texts with a cultural setting we are not familiar with.

Although dialogue in *Losing Battles* is used almost persistently, not everybody is a talker; in fact, there are two protagonists who do not belong to the talking family group at all.[12] Both are women, and both are schoolteachers. The former is Julia Mortimer, the schoolteacher of Banner community, who has just died, but nevertheless belongs to the family reunion because everybody talks about her; the latter is Gloria Renfro, who was supposed to succeed Julia Mortimer, but gave up her profession in order to marry Jack Renfro, Granny's great-grandson. Julia Mortimer is considered to be "the heart of the novel":[13] she was the Banner schoolteacher, and as such, she has influenced most of the people gathered at Granny's birthday party. Since "she wanted everything brought out in the wide open, to see and be known,"[14] it is at first surprising that Eudora Welty should not have given her any opportunity to articulate her ideas and plans herself. As stated above, Welty intended dialogue to function as a device that would "make everything shown," and now she has a protagonist who is "silent" but whose voice, in an indirect manner, is of crucial importance for the novel. This apparent contradiction calls for particular attention, especially because Gloria Renfro, Julia's protégée, is not a talker either. Gloria participates in the family reunion and in the talks, but her utterances are different from the others'. Like her teacher Julia, Gloria takes an outsider's position amongst the Vaughn-Renfros merely through the special way she contributes to the constant conversation.

If Eudora Welty chose speech in order to reveal "the characters' minds and hearts" why did she then create two female protagonists who do not fit in this pattern of talkers? In what respect do their sex and profession determine their being outsiders? A close analysis of the speech acts of the talkers and Gloria, and a characterization of Julia (as described by the talkers and Gloria and as she presents herself through her written record) will provide insights into the complex design of *Losing Battles*.

But before these speech acts can be analyzed, we have to consider some of the problems that arise when applying speech act theory to literary texts. Speech act theory was originally developed with "natural" discourse, which, unlike fictional discourse, is referential. A speech act can be performed on three different levels: the locutionary act denotes the stating of a sentence in English (or any natural language) according to the rules of English grammar; the illocutionary act has the function of "informing, ordering, warning, undertaking, &c., i.e. utterances which have a certain conventional force." The perlocutionary act describes the consequences upon an interlocutor of a sentence such as "convincing, persuading, deterring."[15] Susan Sniader Lanser emphasizes that speech acts in literary texts are only imitations of speech acts, therefore, "they have no illocutionary force except within the fictional world."[16] And since literary speech acts have no illocutionary force they have no perlocutionary effects either. Yet Lanser and also Mary Pratt, who discusses speech act theory in literary discourse in great detail,[17] do not concentrate on the speech acts of characters vis-à-vis other characters in the text. They are concerned with the speech act between the narrator and his/her narrative audience because then one can speak of a "real" communication, namely between the text and the reader.

John R. Searle also comments on illocutionary acts in fiction and he concludes that the illocutionary act performed when a sentence is uttered is usually a function of the meaning of the sentence.

> Anyone therefore who wishes to claim that fiction contains different illocutionary acts from nonfiction is committed to the view that words do not have their normal meanings in works of fiction.[18]

Seymour Chatman sees in the theory of speech acts a useful tool for the analysis of the narrator's language and of the one of characters vis-à-vis each other. Unfortunately, he mainly focuses on the narrator's speech acts and only states that the speech acts of characters contain "a wider range of illocutions" because they "directly interact with other characters, not with the narratee and/or implied reader."[19] Richard Ohmann applies speech act theory to literary discourse,[20] yet, he, too, maintains that "[l]iterary works are discourses with the usual rules suspended, acts without consequences of the usual sort" and that "the writer puts out imitation speech acts *as if* they were being performed by someone."[21] But he nevertheless makes clear that speech act theory provides necessary tools for an approach to literature viewed as being political. He brings up the importance of the reader's participation in a text consisting of illocutions stating that the reader always makes judgments based on his/her own knowledge of "the conditions for happily performing illocutionary acts."[22] A reader re-enacts the imitated speech acts in a written literary work. A reader's participation in this transaction varies and is dependent on gender, class, race, age, income, and his/her social and personal past.[23]

Re-enacting speech acts necessitates the reader's participation, but it also means the reader's interpretation of the speech acts of characters vis-à-vis each other. Therefore, I consider an analysis of characters' speech acts a legitimate and rewarding undertaking with a text consisting mainly of speech acts of characters and not of narrators. Such a text as *Losing Battles* with its numerous pieces of dialogue indeed contains a wider range of illocutions—and perlocutions—than a text with a narrator telling the story to the reader because a narrator's speech act can only have illocutionary force towards the reader, but not towards another character of the narrative.

## TALK AND GOSSIP IN THE FAMILY

The first speech uttered in *Losing Battles* is already a loud and clear demonstration of the togetherness of the tribal clan: Granny's granddaughter Beulah Renfro mockingly reproaches her grandmother for having got dressed all by herself and not having called for help. All of Beulah's short utterances are emphasized by an exclamation mark, and the very "cry" denotes the loudness. After her encounter with Granny she calls her children; her three daughters appear and their simultaneous "Happy birthday, Granny!" again illustrates the conformity to family rituals and unity. Granny's answer manifests family continuity and generation pride:

"I'm expecting to see all my living grandchildren, all my great-grandchildren, and all the great-great-grandchildren. . . . I'm a hundred today" (p. 5). This utterance is immediately followed by Beulah's command to one of her daughters not to contradict her although, as we know, they are celebrating Granny's ninetieth birthday.

The next longer conversation among the Renfro family has as its topic the sequence of appearances of the other family members who will all celebrate Granny's birthday. Their conjectures refer to all kinds of reasons why a certain uncle might be late or another will be first (cf. p. 13). Welty meticulously records speeches that, on the surface, seem meaningless or unnecessary for our information on other characters. As Louis Rubin points out, "[e]verything is out on the surface, but the art *is* the surface, and every inch of the surface must be inspected,"[24] and one realizes that this surface is characteristic of the conversations. They throw light on the life of Banner community, they reveal the daily struggle of the family. These speeches have the illocutionary force of informing or asking questions. Confronted with this constant chatting, the reader "listens" intensely and thus tends to be included in the situation, but the mere fact of his/her being impelled to listen while *reading* impedes the process of inclusion.

An illustrative example of the structure of these conversations is Uncle Percy's account of the story of why Jack Renfro was sent to prison. Although Percy is the teller of the tale, the other members of the family participate in the talk by commenting, asking questions, correcting, or deviating from the actual content of the story. At times, Percy even loses the floor as a speaker because the others provide so much information themselves. Aunt Cleo, who has just married a Beecham and is thus a newcomer to the family, asks questions about the family history. Jack's sister Ella Fay, who was present when Jack got entangled in his fight with the storekeeper (the reason why he was put into prison), relives part of the role she played by giving her very personal account of the events. Percy's use of the present tense and of the direct speeches of the characters involved enhance the immediacy and the dramatic impact of the story. Although some of the listeners have heard this story before, they all participate as if it were entirely new.

The homogenous circle of speaker and listeners indicates how family oriented they are: they all take Jack's side and criticize his antagonist, Curly. This similarity of behavior makes it difficult for the reader to differentiate between the talkers, to recognize their individual traits, and to attribute specific characteristics to the speakers.[25] Moreover, their additional comments do not show a very personal coloring.

At the very beginning of the family gathering it becomes clear that Gloria is an outsider. Her special status within the family is expressed in her very first speech act: after Jack's three sisters have called her for breakfast, she explains to them that she is busy and they should "go on without [her and her baby]" (p. 7). Gloria's utterance has perlocutionary force because it entails an effect on her interlocutors: they must remain without Gloria and her daughter. When she first appears she does not speak, whereas the various aunts are eager to articulate their judgments of Gloria, and to let her know what they think of her dress or hair. Their statements are mere illocutions: they give judgments, comments, or ask questions. One of the aunts even states that Gloria looks as if she "stepped out of a storybook" (p. 14). This is a remarkable comment since Gloria is the only character, apart from Julia Mortimer, who does not tell stories herself and who appears to be the most "real" character of the book in the sense that she does not believe in the "unrealistic" concept of time the reunion shares. Talking about the different concepts of time in *Losing Battles*, Michael Kreyling points out that "the reunion can hold the past within the present, erase unwanted time or events that do not fit into the archetypal pattern."[26] Gloria, on the other hand, is concerned about the future and has no faith in the family's ever-returning stories.

The family's lively interest in Jack's story is an example of their orientation to the past, creating the past anew while telling the same story for perhaps the third time. In spite of the repetitive elements of the same story-telling there is a development in the conversation: the discussion of Jack's encounter with Curly evokes another story, namely how Jack became Gloria's husband. Again Gloria is more or less silent as the aunts tell Aunt Cleo, the most inquisitive one, their version of Jack and Gloria's meeting. Gloria's reticence within the family circle has already been mentioned; it becomes more understandable in her later conversation with Jack when she tells him about Julia Mortimer's advice not to marry him because this would only bring her "trouble and hardship" (p. 169).

The initial speech acts in *Losing Battles* are quite straightforward and unambiguous; as a whole they reveal a tightly knit clan that will eventually become more dominant the larger the reunion grows. The speech acts also illustrate that Gloria does not consider herself to be part of this homogenous circle. Her communicative behavior is different when she is alone with Jack. Their first long serious talk together is, as mentioned above, about Julia Mortimer's warning. An analysis of Gloria's and Jack's conversation shows that the previous short pieces of dialogue among the Beechams, Vaughns, and Renfros are loosely knit together: one piece does not necessarily develop a further piece. The young couple's speech acts, on the other hand, contain an unbroken thread. Gloria and Jack both concentrate on each other's statements and their answers are logical results of the foregoing statement. None of their utterances evokes a tall tale as it is the case within the family circle. They concentrate on one specific topic and try to discuss the issue of Gloria's relation to Julia Mortimer. Immediate reactions to an opinion are directly expressed, sometimes in a physical manifestation ("He gripped her," p. 169; "Gloria's tears ran down," p. 170). The reader gets the impression that two people are really talking together, whereas in the midst of the large family circle one is talking and the others are listening or interfering and thus changing the course of the story being told. Yet, direct consequences of the speaker's illocutions for the listeners cannot be noted.

There is an obvious difference between the gossiping family members of the reunion and Gloria and Jack: for most family members talking seems to be a way of coping with their daily problems. But they do not talk in order to analyze or discuss these problems as Jack and Gloria do; talking helps them to survive in their daily struggle to get enough food and clothing, and to keep a modest house (cf. the numerous references to the new roof). This strategy of survival is especially effective within the family community, in which repetition, assertion, and loyalty[27] play an important role. Communicating these attitudes to each other provides the family members with a feeling of inclusion and safety, which they otherwise cannot experience because their material situation is not safe at all. Speech is the essential factor in creating stability in an unstable world, in which fighting battles means "losing battles."

Jack's and Gloria's speech behavior encompasses more than a strategy of survival; especially Gloria vividly shows that she wants to express a certain opinion or position and that she depends on the reactions of her listener(s). Thus, Gloria produces speech acts that have effects on her audience; they are frequently perlocutions. The following chapter will concentrate on Gloria's and Julia's outsider positions and on the characteristics of Gloria's speech behavior.

## THE SCHOOLTEACHERS JULIA AND GLORIA: A VOICE OF THEIR OWN

Julia Mortimer never participates in any conversations in the novel, but she has been given a voice whose importance surpasses that of the actual talkers. Julia dies on the day of the great reunion. With her death, she paradoxically becomes a member of the reunion because, as it turns out, she has exercised an influence on almost everybody present at the gathering and people start remembering their relationships with the schoolteacher. Significantly, the very first mention of Julia in the book comes from Gloria, Julia's student and potential successor at Banner School. It is Gloria who tells Aunt Cleo about Miss Julia Mortimer, whose place she was supposed to take. Like Miss Eckhart in *The Golden Apples*, who is disappointed by her pupil Virgie, Julia had to accept that her pupil envisaged another future than teaching. Thus, already at the beginning of the novel, we learn about a lost battle with regard to the teacher's aims.

Since Julia Mortimer never speaks for herself, the reader must rely entirely on the other characters' opinions about her. Gloria's statements differ a great deal from the family's, and, as mentioned above, Gloria is most articulate about this issue when she is alone with Jack. She refers to her as "Saint George," a name the teacher gave herself to express her position as a fighter of battles. Gloria is even more explicit in describing Julia's battles: instead of fighting the dragon Julia had to fight ignorance (p. 245). The reference to the slaying of the dragon reminds us of Miss Eckhart's picture of Perseus and Medusa, of which the teacher used to say that it is "the same thing as Siegfried and the Dragon" (*The Golden Apples*, p. 243). A teacher, like Julia, she is fascinated by a heroic act not necessarily the one executed by Perseus. Yet, Miss Eckhart cannot fulfill a heroic deed; she is not even successful with her favorite pupil, Virgie, whom she has chosen to become a piano player like herself. Julia Mortimer's wish to have Gloria as her successor is similar to Miss Eckhart's goal, but she must also learn that her pupil does not consider her wishes. Yet, Julia's fight against ignorance is partly successful all the same: there are many people in the Banner community who have been affected by Julia in some ways: lawyers, doctors, and teachers now living away from Banner are the intellectual offspring of Julia Mortimer.

Julia Mortimer is not only an influential character as a schoolteacher; even after her death she articulates her wishes.

In her testament, written into a speller, she wants everybody who once attended her classes to be present at her funeral. Moreover, she determinedly expresses her wish to be buried under the schoolhouse. Her written testament indeed contains a perlocutionary act: the people listening to its reading are irritated by her request. Aunt Beulah Renfro aptly points out that "she hasn't given up yet. . . . Trying to regiment the reunion into being part of her funeral" (p. 292). Other family members also indirectly refer to Julia's battle (against ignorance), but their comments only partly characterize the schoolteacher.

In spite of the dominance of dialogue in the novel, it is a written statement that expresses Julia's concern precisely and most informatively. It is a striking feature that in a novel consisting mostly of dialogues the written text should be correlated with a teacher: the schoolteacher's battle against ignorance has a lot to do with books, reading, and writing in general. Julia's last message for the people she wanted to teach is in the medium they mostly suspect as being "strange": "She read in the daytime. . . . And that was a thing surpassing strange for a well woman to do" (p. 294). This comment about a woman reading reminds us of many gifted nineteenth-century heroines who were not allowed to live a life according to their intellectual faculties. Maggie Tulliver's yearning for books and knowledge is a case in point; the dictum by her brother's (male) teacher that girls have "a great deal of superficial cleverness" and therefore are "quick and shallow"[28] reflects the sexist view regarding female intelligence. Neither are Julia Mortimer's intellect and deep vocation for educating people understood in the Banner community. As Julia writes in a letter to Judge Moody, a former student of hers, who reads the letter at the reunion, she has lost almost every battle because the children at Banner School "took up the cause of the other side and held the fort against me" (p. 298). In spite of this antagonism she kept on fighting, her strength being her belief that she could implement a change in the future.

The written word has not been a successful weapon in

Julia's "hard war with ignorance" (p. 298), but it proves to be effective all the same: even after her death she has a voice at the reunion, and everybody is compelled to listen to her words, although they are not uttered by herself. The transmission of her last wish, necessarily in the medium of the written word, is bound to be heard because it is read to the reunion as at a public gathering. The members of the reunion express their discord or astonishment at what they hear in the course of the reading. Some comments even have an intensifying effect for the reader because he/she is referred back to Julia's text again: when Aunt Beulah learns that Julia has lived "by naked inspiration" (p. 298), her reaction "I wish we didn't have to hear it" (p. 299) makes us reconsider Julia's statements. The written word, in the end, weighs more heavily than the endless conversations; indeed, it underlines the aim of the book as such: the novel must be *read*, and only the written medium makes the rendering of the dialogues possible. The talkers' stance and influence are weakened due to the impact of the written word, whereas Julia's testament and letter have more (perlocutionary) force.

Thus, Julia Mortimer's insistent battle against ignorance cannot be considered a "lost battle" as she herself states; perhaps it is a losing battle and her fighting has never really come to an end because her belief that everything must be "brought out in the wide open, to see and be known" proves to be true for her own last written statement. Peggy Prenshaw compares her battle to Saint George's or Perseus's, and even speaks of an "aggressive, masculine advance against monstrous Nature, which brutishly accepts or forgives, or ignores individual victory or death."[29] This "aggressive, masculine advance" is also pertinent to Virgie, whose attempt to be "heroic" shares traits with the freedom-loving, forward-going hero. Like Julia Mortimer, Virgie not only lives for the present, but also cares about the future. We will later see that Gloria is equally concerned about the future; in this respect she seems to be influenced by her teacher Julia.

It is interesting to note that Peggy Prenshaw interprets

the fighting attitude as "masculine." Being aggressive and moving forward is thus associated with the male domain as is the hero's search for the heroic deed, which we have observed in the last chapter. Julia Mortimer's "male" characteristic of fighting battles against ignorance makes her (ignorant) opponents even more suspicious: a woman with a strong will who is "full of books" (p. 240) "ought to have married somebody. . . . Then what she wanted wouldn't mean a thing. She would be buried with him, and no questions asked" (p. 296). This last statement by one of the aunts refers to Julia's wish to be buried under the schoolhouse and is indicative of the family reunion's expectations that an unmarried woman, let alone a thinking and educated woman, is troublesome in any case.

Although Julia loses her battle for her own burial ground, she manages posthumously to gather people for her funeral. Many of her former pupils arrive from all over the country to bid her good-bye. The funeral, covered in the last few pages of *Losing Battles*, is mainly reported to us in descriptive passages. The gossiping tone has disappeared and there is only a longer piece of dialogue between Gloria and Jack, which brings the story to an end. As in *The Golden Apples* the novel concludes with a funeral; in *Losing Battles* it is the burial of a protagonist who has never uttered a word in the novel except indirectly through her letter and testament. It seems only right that her funeral and the close of the book should coincide: she who represents books and knowledge in general is buried; the book cannot continue without Julia. Her effort to have "everything brought out in the wide open" and to have people "spread out their minds and hearts to other people, so they could be read like books" (p. 432) becomes futile if there is no medium such as a book. In this respect the battle is not over only for Julia, the teacher, but also for the writer and reader of the novel. It remains open whether the reader feels defeated in a lost battle, or whether he/she will continue Julia's battle against ignorance.

As already mentioned, Julia's protégée Gloria does not

continue her teacher's battle, but she shares certain attitudes with her all the same. As mentioned before, Gloria's speech behavior characterizes her as an outsider among the family clan. She is reticent about herself and does not participate in the story-telling. Even Aunt Beulah, her mother-in-law, complains that "you can't read her" (p. 69). It is almost ironical that she uses the verb "read" since she and her family are most suspicious of people who read.

Gloria's outsider position is not only determined by her speech behavior, but also by her origin; she is an orphan, and there are various assumptions about her parents. Being an orphan like Easter in *The Golden Apples* similarly implies exclusion and vulnerability.[30] It is characteristic of the clan's credo that they quite forcefully urge Gloria to "say Beecham" (p. 269) and accept the fact that she is one of them. The aunts brutally stuff a piece of sticky watermelon into Gloria's mouth to ritually endorse their claim.[31] Throughout the book Gloria insists again and again that she is "nobody's kin" and "[her] own boss" (p. 315). A great number of her utterances refer to her independent status and her wish to be alone with Jack and her baby and to move to a house of their own, instead of living with Jack's "family piled all over him" (p. 163). Seymour Gross interprets Gloria's endeavor to live an independent life as "an almost neurotic concern for herself" and "a penchant for self-dramatization that verges on the ludicrous".[32] I think we should take Gloria's anxious concern for independence and privacy seriously and accept her urge to get away from the possessive family clan. Moreover, Gloria, as Julia Mortimer's student, believes in the future as much as she does and cannot cope with the clan's "old dead past" (p. 361). Her consciousness is historical like Julia's,[33] and her looking forward to tomorrow's problems reveals a mind that is not at all self-centered but critical and thoughtful. The family's attitude towards the past is representative of the old South in that its members are primarily concerned with heroic tales about the past, including the Civil War. The parodic tinge inherent in the author's presentation of their tales contributes to the critical stance both Julia and Gloria take regarding this narrow view of time, that is, focusing primarily on the past.[34]

As a former teacher Gloria is "not afraid of pencil and paper" (p. 91), which she used in order to communicate with Jack while he was in prison. Writing is communication for Gloria; she does not believe in the clan's talking. As she tells Jack, "they are just sitting and listening to 'emselves talk" (p. 133). Similar to Julia Mortimer, who makes use of the written word even after her death, Gloria relies on language consciously. She mistrusts the constant story-telling and only speaks when she really wants to make an important statement or, quite frequently, to emphasize her outsider position. She has the courage to stand up to the whole family and to prevent them from accompanying her and Jack. Her utterance is an explicit order to the clan not to interfere in her and Jack's privacy and thus has a decisive effect on her interlocutors.

Although Gloria uses language consciously, the impulse for her thoughts and actions comes from her heart: "I go by what I feel in my heart of hearts" (p. 315). Her statement reminds us of Julia's letter to Judge Moody, in which the teacher confesses that she lives by inspiration (cf. p. 298). It seems as if inspiration and the heart stand in opposition to all the talking and story-telling of the clan. Julia fights her battle at school, Gloria hers at home. It remains open whether Gloria will win her battle and will live an independent life with Jack and their child. She has not heeded her teacher's warning not to get married, and now she is haunted by Julia's letter, which is "still in words of fire on [her] brain" (p. 314). Like Virgie's "fire in [her] head," the words of fire on Gloria's brain reveal a deep emotional disposition. Virgie's fire, of course, is much stronger than Gloria's because Virgie decisively sets off on her journey for self-fulfillment all by herself, without being impeded by family bonds.

## THE UNHEROIC HERO JACK AND OTHER MALE LOSERS OF THE BATTLE

Gloria's husband Jack is often considered to be the hero[35] of the novel because he escapes from prison just in time to be present at his grandmother's birthday celebration or because he saves Judge Moody's car by putting his life at stake. Yet in spite of the several allusions to the Good Samaritan[36] Jack does not meet the expectations of a hero if we compare him to Julia and Gloria, the two female protagonists. They critically question their social and cultural environments, whereas Jack never does. Moreover, he cannot separate himself from his clan and must be reminded again and again by Gloria that he should first think of his wife and child. Commenting on Jack as a hero, Mary Anne Ferguson relies on Ihab Hassan's definition of "radical innocence" in order to describe Jack's affirmative attitude.[37] Viewed within the tradition of the comic epic, Ferguson argues, Jack is an innocent, "naive and foolish"[38] hero. I would, however, argue more strongly than even Peggy Prenshaw, who states that he is "perhaps not a hero at all";[39] he is definitely no hero compared to Julia Mortimer, who has decisive battles to fight. Jack is confronted with the kind of adventures that belong to the chivalric world, and his sufferings are not as existential as Julia Mortimer's and are limited in time.

Although Jack is not a superficial talker, he does not use language as consciously as Gloria or Julia do. He carefully listens to Gloria's utterances and shows great sympathy for Julia. He is proud of his family ties and cannot quite see Gloria's reservations about them. But we may assume that Gloria will be capable of realizing her wish of "a little house to [them]selves" where "nobody could ever find [them]" and they would be safe from "the whole reunion solid behind [them]" (p. 171). Jack is not a dominating husband, as his speech behavior shows. He frequently comforts Gloria and mostly acts in her interests (e.g., he promises to take her to Julia's funeral). As mentioned above, he and Gloria can develop an argument in the course of their conversation, whereas the other members of the Beecham-Vaughn-Renfro clan usually deviate from a specific topic and cling to their tale-telling. Most of his utterances are illocutions without perlocutionary force. His "acts" with consequences for other people such as escaping from the state prison or pulling out Judge Moody's car from a roadside ditch belong to the physical realm.

In this sense, differences in speech behavior seem to depend not only on the degree of involvement in the clan or on an outsider position; they are also related to the sex of the speaker. The male talkers[40] often take the lead in the longer story-telling episodes: Uncle Percy is the teller of the story, which expounds the reasons for Jack's imprisonment, and Uncle Curtis and Brother Bethune dominate the family's recollections of their past (cf. pp. 177–185). The women generally refrain from giving longer comments; they often provide additional information in short exclamations.[41] This gender-specific speech behavior only illustrates male dominance on the level of story-telling (by the characters); it actually contrasts with the important positions the women hold in *Losing Battles*: Julia Mortimer, Granny Vaughn, and Aunt Beulah, who is the head of the family now that Granny is old and fragile. As M. E. Bradford points out, "this novel is, like the tale of Shellmound, a 'woman's novel.' "[42]

*Losing Battles* as a "woman's book" especially illustrates how two women fight battles against a community and a family clan. Their outsider position is mainly marked by their "silent" attitude in a book that consists predominantly of dialogue. This narrative strategy concentrates the reader's attention on these characters. The numerous characters talking along weigh much less against the silent schoolteacher and the reticent Gloria. In *Delta Wedding* women's supremacy takes place within a narrative realm; in *Losing Battles* it manifests itself through a specific speech behavior that reflects a powerful use of language and silence. Julia Mortimer, though dead and silent, keeps on fighting a battle by means of the written word so that a whole family is bound to listen to her. Gloria Renfro tries to separate herself from the clan by articulating her needs and wishes very explicitly. Although she is no longer a teacher, she is a follower of Julia Mortimer in that she uses language in order to *act*. In terms of speech act theory, both Julia and Gloria mostly perform a perlocutionary speech act, whereas most of the other speakers' utterances are illocutionary speech acts. The function of perlocution defined as producing consequences or effects on the audience is pertinent to Gloria's and Julia's speech acts.

*Losing Battles* is not only a novel about battles, it is, above all, a novel about (speech) acts. Although Welty emphasizes her intention to "translat[e] every thought and feeling into action and speech" (cf. above), the two nontalkers exercise more power in their acts and actions than the talkers. The most effective weapon on the battlefield is the language used by the two women protagonists—and by their "creatress."[43]

# 5

# *The Optimist's Daughter*: A Woman's Memory

## MEMORY AND TIME

In her novel following *Losing Battles* Eudora Welty returns to the narrative mode of conveying mainly interior events through her characters. In her most recent autobiographical book, *One Writer's Beginnings*,[1] she describes this "inward journey that leads us through time":

> As we discover, we remember; remembering, we discover; and most intensely do we experience this when our separate journeys converge. Our living experience at those meeting points is one of the charged dramatic fields of fiction. (*OWB*, p. 102)

This statement leads Welty to a passage from *The Optimist's Daughter* in which the protagonist Laurel Hand *remembers* the moment when she and her husband saw the confluence of the Ohio and Mississippi rivers. Confluence "exists as a reality and a symbol in one" (*OWB*, p. 102); it connotes all our inward journeys coming together, and, as Welty concludes her autobiographical work, "the greatest confluence of all is that which makes up the human memory—the individual human memory" (*OWB*, p. 104). In our memory our experiences—normally submitted to a sequential order—can be grasped at one and the same moment. Through remembering we realize our being alive, and since we can only remember something that has passed already, time is the most essential element linked with memory. Talking about time in fiction, Welty refers to Faulkner's famous statement that "[m]emory believes before knowing remembers,"[2] and she also insists on the inevitable need of remembering one's past: "Remembering is done through the blood, it is a bequeathment. . . . It is also a life's work."[3] It is only logical that Welty also mentions Faulkner's *The Sound and the Fury*, in which time is different for the three first-person narrators and their respective stories; thus, Faulkner presents "three different worlds of memory."[4]

In Nabokov's novel *Ada, or Ardor: A Family Chronicle* the memoirist of the book defines time and memory as interrelated: "Time is but memory in the making."[5] Everything that *is* already belongs to the past when we remember it, and it is always experienced differently according to the person who remembers. In *The Optimist's Daughter* the reader is confronted with the world of a middle-aged woman's memory. As the title explicitly says, she is also a daughter, and I suggest that she has reminiscences specifically linked with a female world. Considering the fact that time is traditionally related to paternal thinking in terms of the "genealogical imperative,"[6] the woman's memories might express a specific relationship to Father Time. The concept of linear time follows the patriarchal pattern in Western culture, which consists of "the prestige of the father over the son."[7] Thus, the line of time is conceived of as something that is directed towards an aim and also reflects an authority (father-son).[8]

In *Time and the Novel*, Patricia Tobin describes how the twentieth-century novel in particular tries to subvert the linear dominance by disrupting the chronology of time and to get rid of the "genealogical imperative." Among her examples is Gabriel Garcia Marquez's *One Hundred Years of Solitude*, which is characterized by a return "to myth, to nature, to magic, to the mother."[9] With the disappearance of the father (the murder of the father) the patrilinear narrative is no longer given.

I shall not set out to determine whether Welty's *The Optimist's Daughter* has a specific function in this tendency to displace the father, but I shall concentrate on the aspects of time and memory in a woman writer's creation of a female character. Julia Kristeva quotes James Joyce's "Father's time, mother's species" to emphasize that *woman* is more frequently linked with "the space generating and forming the human species" than with time. But she points out that the history of civilization shows "two types of temporality (cyclical and monumental) . . . traditionally linked to female subjectivity."[10] In *The Optimist's Daughter* the female protagonist is the one who remembers and who relates to time more than any of the other characters. It is therefore pertinent to raise the question whether time is transformed into a female sphere and if so, how this transformation manifests itself.

Like time, memory, too, can have a specific function for *woman*. Mary Daly mentions memory as a device for women to tell the truth about their lives.[11] She refers to Virginia Woolf, who, as a writer, was very consciously aware of the power of memory:

> She was/is a Muse, singing other women into conscious Memory, a Soothsayer whose creative pursuit of the past overcame impotence and paralysis, actualizing

> potency. Intuitively she knew that the passive potency to hear/see/receive knowledge of the Background is interconnected with active potency to Name, for "it is only by putting it into words that I make it [reality] whole."[12]

Woolf's insistence on the existential importance of memory draws our attention to Welty's statement that remembering is essential for staying alive. For both writers the process of writing "actualizes Memory in an especially potent way."[13] It is probably not coincidental that Virginia Woolf is a "precursor" for Welty with respect to memory; as Welty herself states, Woolf "was the one who opened the door."[14] Indeed, reading Welty's works one is often reminded of Woolf's psychological presentation of characters.[15] One of the themes of *The Optimist's Daughter* also appears in Woolf's *To the Lighthouse*. Michael Kreyling, dedicating a whole chapter to a comparison of these two novels, especially emphasizes the "idea of distance, whether the distance is created by the passing of time or by the gulf between the self and the public role, self and society, self and loved one, and self and the truth."[16]

While I mention Virginia Woolf in connection with memory, I must also refer to the importance of the mother-daughter relationship, which plays a crucial role in Welty's novel. It is again in *To the Lighthouse* that Woolf explores aspects of this essential female realm. Both Welty's and Woolf's novels are examples of a women writers' tradition: "the excavation of buried plots in women's texts has revealed an enduring, if recessive, narrative concern with the story of mothers and daughters."[17] Therefore I shall especially focus on this mother-daughter narrative and compare it to the description of the father-daughter relationship. As the title indicates, the book is also about a father, the optimist, and his daughter. Although "optimist," in English, could also refer to a woman, the reference to the father becomes clear after a few pages of reading. Yet, as the following chapters will elucidate, the "buried plot" of the mother-daughter story could suggest a different title of the book since it lies at the core of the book.

## LAUREL HAND: THE DAUGHTER OF AN OPTIMIST

Laurel McKelva Hand's father, Judge McKelva, has eye trouble, and therefore undergoes an examination in New Orleans where his daughter meets him. He tells his doctor friend that there is "something wrong with [his] *eyes.*"[18] This very first dialogue of the book expresses an anxiety about not *seeing* well. This deficiency of sight already indicates a problem in perceiving one's surroundings. It does not concern Judge McKelva exclusively, but he is the most obvious example of a blind man, both literally and figuratively. His second marriage to Fay, a woman who does not show much understanding of his sufferings and who has an entirely different social background, seems to be an escape from his loneliness after the death of his first wife, Becky.

Not only is McKelva's eyesight waning, his "*memory* had slipped" (p. 5) too, as he himself states, when he did not remember that one should not prune a climber before it blooms. He noticed his eye trouble for the first time after pruning roses and therefore assumed that he hurt himself. Yet, the eye specialist assures him that "what happened didn't happen to the outside of his eye, it happened to the inside" (p. 7). This reference to a damaged retina enhances the suggestion of his not having the right vision of things. The retina, sensitive to light, is described as having "slipped" (p. 7),[19] and as a consequence McKelva believes that he sees behind him (cf. p. 5). This impression of seeing behind him is exclusively symbolic because, from a physiological point of view, such an incident is impossible. The bird reflectors McKelva mentions might have evoked an afterimage. His vision is not only impaired with respect to focusing, but also with respect to getting to the kernel of things, that is, the outward as well as the inward look remains dimmed.

After McKelva has undergone eye surgery he is forced to lie totally still. Before the operation he has declared that he is an optimist in reply to the doctor's warning that the operation would not be "a hundred per cent predictable" (p. 10). Yet, during the time of convalescence he develops a less optimistic attitude towards his illness. Laurel, sitting at his bedside, is the observer and indirect recorder of his state of mind: immobile, he no longer shows the curiosity typical of his character and hardly speaks to her or to his wife. Laurel realizes that "what occupied his full mind was time itself; time passing: he was concentrating" (p. 19). McKelva's concern for time is also expressed in his first question in the morning about the exact time. In *Delta Wedding* it is also Laura's father who always wants to know what time it is (cf. *DW*, p. 231). It is indeed "Father's time" that characterizes McKelva's relationship to his surroundings, including his daughter. Laurel is susceptible to her father's preoccupations with time and even sets "her inner chronology with his, more or less as if they needed to keep in step for a long walk ahead of them" (pp. 19–20). She seems to accept her father's pace, recognizing that she cannot influence or alter his concept of time. This insight is crucial, because her father during the long time of her mother's illness always tried to make his wife believe that she might get well soon, thus not accepting the different pace of the dying woman. This information is only given towards the end of the book, when Laurel relives the time of her mother's dying. Laurel's behavior at her father's deathbed must be conceived in relation to her memories of her mother's illness and her father's attitude at his wife's deathbed.

Laurel's mother also suffered from an eye illness, indicated only in some vague and rather mysterious references such as "it's like Mother's" or "the eye was just a part of it" (p. 9). The beginning of her eye trouble was a "little cataract" (p. 145), which was operated on, but Becky's eyesight deteriorated all the same, and she eventually lost it completely. Retrospectively, Laurel realizes how her father could not meet Becky's expectations: he could not accept his wife's illness and therefore "he apparently needed guidance in order to see the tragic" (p. 145). The comfort and hope he bestowed upon his wife contrasted with the actual state of Becky's mental and physical condition. When she desired to be brought back to her beloved mountains in West Virginia, he immediately promised to take her there. Laurel describes his offer as "the first worthless promise that had ever lain between them" (p. 149). Becky, realizing that her husband could not face the fact of her mortality, called him a coward and liar, and we are told that this accusation made him become an optimist (cf. p. 150). Thus, his optimism derives from an inability to accept his wife's approaching death. The narrator does not hesitate to tell us the sheer truth about the relationship between this couple: "It was betrayal on betrayal" (p. 150) because McKelva caused Becky's desperation by not acknowledging her desperation.

Becky died without speaking a word, lonely and "keeping everything to herself, in exile and humiliation" (p. 151); in this respect her husband follows her mode of resignation because he, too, stops communicating. Laurel is aware of his concentration and she even tries to help him to go along with "time." She comforts him once by assuring him that he will soon be able to wear his spectacles, but she immediately recognizes the potential insincerity of her statement.[20] Thus, Laurel is aware of her father's actual condition and does not deceive him by false promises.

The recollection of her mother's deathbed only occurs after her father's death, that is, the memories are not narrated at the time of her father's dying or immediately after his death. Only after the funeral can Laurel explore the true nature of her memories regarding her parents, and at a moment of epiphany, a recognition of the ambivalent character of her parents' relationship, she is capable of facing her mother's ordeal retrospectively.

Laurel's reminiscing is significantly triggered by the book titles she peruses when she enters her father's library. The library is—and always was—his domain. The room is described from Laurel's point of view by a third-person narrator with access to Laurel's memories. The perspective of the daughter in her father's library focuses on the portraits of her father's father and grandfather, her father's great-grandfather's desk, with the papers he had kept when he was mayor of Mount Salus, and with numerous files and folders. All these items strongly reflect a male spirit. The traditionally male realm is enforced by references to lawbooks or even a telescope (we recall Loch's viewing through the telescope, which I identified as typically male in contrast to Cassie's more encompassing "view"). This male atmosphere sharply contrasts with the description of "the woman's room" of Laurel's mother, with which the reader is confronted when Laurel enters her mother's sewing room.

Laurel's memories about her father unveil other characteristics mostly pertinent to men who are intellectually absorbed by their exacting work: such men, although experts in their fields, often have a narrow view with regard to human relationships. Looking out of the window Laurel perceives her long-time neighbor, the town teacher Miss Adele Courtland, who, as Laurel now realizes, waves toward the window as she used to when she hoped to catch a glance from Judge McKelva looking out the window. Laurel is certain that her father never saw the woman who quietly loved him. The reference to impaired vision is again both literal and figurative; McKelva, trying his best to serve his town as a judge, does not even recognize his neighbor's feelings towards him. He only sees what fits into his daily pattern of correct procedure. We have observed the same incapacity to adjust his vision when Becky is mortally ill. Laurel's insight into her father's oblivion regarding his surroundings seems possible only now that she can reminisce with a critical stance. Her exact viewing of her father's room enables her to understand her father's past life more accurately, too.

Approaching the desk, Laurel at first hesitates, but then opens every drawer to look for the letters her mother had written to her husband when they were separated. Confronted with completely empty drawers, she realizes that her father had never kept any letters. He had been careful to erase all written traces of a past moment in correspondence, whereas her mother had kept all of her husband's letters. Laurel, with obvious disappointment, must accept that "there was nothing of her mother here for Fay to find, or for herself to retrieve" (p. 123). The distance between Laurel and her father, which already began to grow at the hospital, now seems to be a more delicate problem to surmount. Michael Kreyling states that "Laurel contends with the issues of distance in human relationships, with memory, and with faith in human life";[21] only the right connections may help to bring together, that is, to achieve a confluence of the single aspects of life. The catalyst of such a process is the right vision.[22] There is a compelling need to try and grasp the sense-making links of one's history, of one's past, present, and future. For Laurel, who used to idealize her parents and her dead husband, a new in*sight* is necessary. Now, confronted with her father's death, she begins a new phase of her life: after her parents' and her husband's deaths she seems to have torn the last thread with her idealized past. She is bound to rely entirely on her memory in order to relive past moments.

Exploring her father's library after his death is an attempt to relive some of her and her father's past through its material evidence. But instead of discovering some token of the past, Laurel must realize that there is indeed nothing left in the library except the books, which make her recall the voices of her parents reading them aloud. But these memories relate to both father and *mother*. Ironically enough, the only trace Laurel finds is Fay's nail polish, which she is eager to clean off her father's desk. Thus, Laurel leaves her father's room without having discovered any material traces. Not even her memory can bring back to her the relationship with her father. Having entered the library in order to find some sign of the past, Laurel must rub off a sign of the present. As at her father's deathbed, she cannot make the right connection. The visit to her mother's room, the sewing room, discloses more missing links with the past and to Laurel's history. Here, her memory unveils much more than with her father.

At the outset of this chapter I mentioned the traditional concept of Father Time, the patrilinear line in a narrative, and its possible replacement; in our novel, Laurel's relation to time can no longer be called paternal because her father, the person she tries to get back to while in his library, does not appear as the central figure in Laurel's memories. Memory, which makes past moments come back and singles them out according to their significance, seems to turn against the father, that is, the recollections of her father do not appear to be as important as one would expect after the outset of the novel. The symbolic impact of the empty drawers furthermore illustrates how limited Laurel's power of memory is with regard to her father. "The optimist's daughter" is bereft of her father once again after she has literally lost him at the hospital. Her memory does not equally participate in reviving her father as it does when Laurel explores her mother's story.

Welty's intensive narrative concern with a mother-daughter relationship pushes the father into the background. Although the title of the novel suggests an inspection of a father-daughter relationship, we must acknowledge that the issue of relationship is transferred to the mother. As in *Losing Battles*, in which the dead Julia Mortimer exerts an essential influence, Laurel's mother is vividly present in the book although she has already been dead for almost twelve years when the action of the novel begins. Laurel's mother is not only a "silently" influential protagonist like Julia Mortimer, she is also the mother of the actual protagonist, through whose memory she becomes tangible for the reader. Unlike her father, Laurel's mother is made alive again just because of the peculiarity of the mother-daughter relationship. Indeed, "the buried plot" of the mother-daughter relationship (cf. above) is unveiled just after the father has been buried. The power of his daughter's memory with respect to his life is restricted, whereas it evokes life when concerned with the mother. His daughter's memory has a limited power with respect to his life, whereas it is potent enough to be the motor of an extended narration of the mother's life.

## LAUREL: A MOTHER'S DAUGHTER

In her notable and weighty essay on the development of women's identity and the specificity of the mother-daughter relationship, Jane Flax comes to the conclusion that a woman's difficulty in becoming autonomous and independent derives from the intricate relationship with her mother.[23] This relationship influences the development of a woman's core identity and renders it problematic because the girl cannot separate her own identity from her mother's. The necessary process of differentiation[24] is threatened. Jane Flax states the main reasons for the impediment to differentiation: in patriarchal society children are looked after by their mothers, while their fathers usually work and are tied to the public world. The girl,[25] identifying with the mother because of her sex, faces a dilemma if she wants to leave the familial world: should she stay with her mother who nurtures her and to whom she feels tied, or be autonomous like a man and leave her mother (often feeling guilty thereby)?

This fragmentary outline of a psychological problem with which daughters are confronted helps us to grasp some of the aspects of the mother-daughter relationship between Becky and Laurel. As I have mentioned above, this relationship is depicted retrospectively and always from the daughter's point of view. Thus, the effects of the daughter's unconscious experiences dating from the preoedipal period[26] are also inherent in this presentation. The memory shaping Laurel's thoughts and feelings about her mother is already characterized by a very strong tie to her mother just because of the traditional mother role Becky obviously had.

The long, crucial passage dealing with Laurel's relationship to her mother is significantly introduced by Laurel's entering her mother's sewing room. Her contact with her dead mother, which is presented in great detail to us by the narrator, takes place in a realm traditionally attributed to a woman's sphere. The room connecting her father's library with the sewing room is, as the narrator calls it, "her father's and mother's room" (p. 129). It not only connects the two realms of Laurel's parents, it is—on a narratological level—also the link between the passages dealing with the respective memories about her parents. This connecting room now belongs to Fay, towards whom Laurel bears ill feelings because of Fay's assault on her sick father. Laurel does not enter this room deliberately; a bird, being caught in the house, frightens her and makes her escape into it and shut the door. " 'Bird in de house mean death' " (*DW*, p. 159), the family's black servant in *Delta Wedding* observes, a remark Troy repeats to his family. In *The Optimist's Daughter* a carpenter, who wants to help Laurel release the bird, calls it a "sign o' bad luck" (p. 164). Certainly, the trapped chimney swift is symbolically related to Laurel's dead parents, but it refers more specifically to Laurel's attitude to the past: like the bird, who cannot get out of the house,[27] Laurel cannot leave this room because she is too frightened of the bird. In other words, she cannot (yet) bear to face her memories, which are "vulnerable to the living moment" (p. 179). The process of Laurel's recognition and insight begins in this room, where she has locked herself in and where she dares to question her remorseful attitude towards Fay.

Laurel desperately feels the need to tell her dead mother about Fay's attempt to shake her husband the night of his death. Laurel's urge to tell her mother is emphasized by the repeating of "mother" (cf. p. 132). Yet, she soon realizes her morally despicable attitude. This desire nevertheless illustrates how intensely Laurel feels the need to confide in her mother in order to be comforted like a little girl. At this moment of great anxiety she hears the chimney swift bang against the door. Horrified, Laurel recoils and enters the sewing room, which opens out of her parents' room.

The sewing room not only represents a women's realm, it also serves as a refuge for Laurel. Significantly, this room is associated with "firelight and warmth—that was what her memory gave her" (p. 133). Indeed, Laurel's reminiscences connected with this particular room refer to essential childhood experiences such as being lifted out of her bed or sitting on the floor collecting scraps of her mother's cloth. The description of the mother and her daughter together in this room evokes a close, comforting atmosphere.[28] Similarly, in *Delta Wedding* Laura remembers her mother, who made a doll for her; in both cases the action of the mother's sewing is conceived of as a soothing, loving contribution. Therefore, it is understandable that Laurel does not hesitate to approach her mother's secretary (which was moved to this sewing room) as she did before she looked through her father's desk. Moreover, Laurel remembers that her mother's "privacy was keyless" (p. 134); thus, she does not need a key to open her mother's desk. Metaphorically, the strong tie between mother and daughter is not loosened by impeding forces.

Unlike Judge McKelva, who immediately disposed of the letters sent to him, Becky kept all her letters.[29] Laurel realizes that "her mother had stored things according to their time and place . . . not by ABC" (p. 135), with the exception of the letters from her father. Her "mother's time" is closely linked to place; the same correlation is stated by Eudora Welty in her essay "Some Notes on Time in Fiction."[30] Welty acknowledges that place has a quality that human beings can grasp, "it has shape, size, boundaries" whereas time is difficult to comprehend because it is "like the wind of the abstract,"[31] and its pace, which we cannot control, makes it even more inconceivable.[32]

As mentioned above, Laurel's father seemed obsessed with

time while he had to lie still; he concentrated in order to sharpen his awareness of time. Dying, he perhaps recognized that "we are mortal: this is time's deepest meaning,"[33] but this insight dawns upon him only at the end of his life.[34] The scene in the sewing room with Laurel remembering how she and her mother visited her mother's home in West Virginia[35] exposes a different relation to time. It is Laurel's way of remembering that creates an awareness of time specifically related to a woman's world. The reader is confronted with a retrospective view of Laurel as a girl through a third-person narrator. The memories described mostly include impressions, feelings, or direct speeches of Laurel, her mother, and grandmother. The emphasis on these three female characters creates the impression of an almost matriarchal (microcosmic) world, although there are "the boys" (as Becky's brothers are called) who entertain their sister. The following passage is an example of how both the language and the situation reflect a female view:

> Bird dogs went streaking the upslanted pasture through the sweet long grass that swept them as high as their noses. While it was still day on top of the mountain, the light still warm on the cheek, the valley was dyed blue under them. While one of the "boys" was coming up, his white shirt would shine for a long time almost without moving in her sight, like Venus in the sky of Mount Salus, while grandmother, mother, and little girl sat, outlasting the light, waiting for him to climb home. (p. 139)

The unity the three females represent is contrasted with the one "boy" who approaches them. The landscape is in harmony with the three figures sitting in the grass and they perceive the male intruder as a female star set against the sky.[36] We come across a similar portrayal of the male intruder into a female world when Judge McKelva arrives to fetch them home. Interestingly enough, this passage precedes a description of unity between Becky and her nature surroundings from Laurel's point of view:

> Sometimes the top of the mountain was higher than the flying birds. Sometimes even clouds lay down the hill, hiding the treetops farther down. The highest house, the deepest well, the tuning of the strings; sleep in the clouds; Queen's Shoals; the fastest conversations on earth—no wonder her mother needed nothing else!
>
> Eventually her father would come for them—he would be called "Mr. McKelva"; and they would go home on the train. (p. 141)

The distance between the idyllic, harmonious scene and McKelva is already expressed by the formal address "Mr. McKelva." The contrast between the nature descriptions and the husband is enhanced because of their predominantly female imagery: "the deepest well," "the clouds," and particularly "Queen's Shoals"[37] evoke associations with a female body. Ellen Moers quotes Freud's "complicated topography of the female genital parts . . . often represented as *landscapes*"[38] in her exploration of female literary landscapes. Indeed, both passages quoted above also contain images connoting the female body. Moreover, on a figurative level, the male genitals (the treetops)[39] are hidden by the soft, comfortable, round womb represented by the clouds. The female landscape according to Freud, and as Ellen Moers has come across it in many writings by women, is "external, accessible, prominent, uneven terrain, not a hidden passageway or chamber."[40] The female landscape, especially created in connection with Becky, that the reader is confronted with is filtered, we should remember, through Laurel's memory. Although the voice is not Becky's or Laurel's but still the third-person narrator's, the descriptions are presented from Laurel's point of view (the most obvious, linguistic sign of this is the frequent use of "*her* mother"; my emphasis). This narrative perspective including both the mother and the daughter strengthens and enhances the bond between the two.

Laurel's reminiscences about her mother in West Virginia are triggered by her looking at some old photographs of her parents taken at Becky's home, which, as she proudly remembers, were developed by her mother herself. I believe it is not a coincidence that Laurel looks at snapshots "created" by her mother because seeing and remembering are intertwined. We recall Eudora Welty's own snapshot album, *One Time, One Place*, where she states this interrelation in a more general context:

> If exposure is essential, still more so is the reflection. Insight doesn't happen often on the click of the moment, like a lucky snapshot, but comes in its own time and more slowly and from nowhere but within.[41]

The kind of reflection that Welty emphasizes is pertinent to Laurel's attitude towards her past: remembering her and especially also her mother's past she manages to "see" more clearly. The process of gaining insight is indeed slower, as Welty points out, and it does not happen according to a person's wish. Laurel's intense occupation with her mother's past gives evidence of the particular and complex bond between mother and daughter.

Besides the mother-daughter relationship there are various references to the grandmother. Giving an account of the days spent in West Virginia, the narrator all of a sudden reports the death of Becky's mother, which came unexpectedly. The description of Becky's grief vividly conveys a daughter's mournfulness.[42] Laurel recalls "the first time she had ever heard anyone cry uncontrollably except herself" (p. 142), which intensifies the presentation of the mother's grief because it is observed by her own daughter (who, one day, will equally mourn her mother). The fact that the reader is confronted with the deaths of both mothers reinforces the supremacy of the mother-daughter relationship in this novel.

Commenting on *The Optimist's Daughter* in an interview Eudora Welty stated that "the mother was the one who influenced both Laurel and her father. So they both referred back to her."[43] I suggest that it is predominantly Laurel who "refers back" to her mother and less so her father because his memories of his first wife are hardly mentioned.

At fifteen Becky had to travel to Baltimore with her sick father, the first part of the trip on a raft in order to get down the river. He died at the hospital, and Becky had to return home with the coffin. This tragic experience is remembered by Laurel in connection with her mother's own ordeal of sickness. Reminiscing about her mother's father and her own she comes to the conclusion that "neither of us saved our fathers" (p. 144). Although Laurel comprehends that in the end nobody can be saved by anybody, this statement not only rings of self-reproach, it also implies an ever-returning cycle for daughters. The letters Laurel finds in the last pigeonhole of her mother's desk are a further link in the essential chain between mother and daughter: these letters were sent to Laurel's mother by her own mother after Becky had left West Virginia. The written evidence of this close bond is represented precisely by the rereading of these letters by the granddaughter.[44] Writing and reading letters, addressed to daughters, is a (written) expression of the matrilinear narrative line discernible throughout the novel. Laurel's mother's and grandmother's written texts are the material evidences of the matrilinear narrative.

In *Losing Battles* the written word is also connected with an influential female character: we recall the schoolteacher Julia Mortimer, remembered by the community mainly because she has given (written) expression to her wishes after her death. The profession of schoolteacher is pertinent to such female characters: Becky was a devoted schoolteacher herself before marrying Judge McKelva. Miss Eckhart in *The Golden Apples* is a further example of a prominent schoolteacher in Welty's novels, although Miss Eckhart is less successful than Julia Mortimer at exercising influence on her pupils.[45] These schoolteachers do not resemble the poor and badly paid Victorian governesses who occupied "an ambiguous and ill-defined no-woman's land"[46] and whose dismal existences have been depicted especially by nineteenth-century women novelists. These Weltian schoolteachers are self-supporting women and, to some extent, have power over the next generation. The description of Becky McKelva as both schoolteacher and mother conveys the belief in writing and books that also leaves its imprint on her daughter. Furthermore, her daughter is named after the state flower of West Virginia (the big laurel), her beloved mother country; thus, the mother names her daughter according to *her* history.

Books play an equally important role during Becky's long illness, and Laurel's memory returns to the hours she spent at her mother's bedside hearing Becky recite whole parts of her mother's favorite *McGuffey's Fifth Reader.* A part of a poem is printed in the book (p. 147); it is the part that Laurel hears in her mind while remembering her mother's recitation. The poem is Robert Southey's "The Cataract of Lodore." It is pertinent to the context of the novel for two reasons: first, the reference to cataract, denoting both the waterfall and the clouding of the eye's lens, thus also referring to a dimmed vision, which plays such an essential role in this book. Second, the poem with its nursery rhyme form is meant to be read to children and thus represents a further sign of the closeness and dependence between mother and little girl. Furthermore, the poem printed on the page contrasts sharply with the empty desk of Laurel's father. In her mother's room Laurel both finds and reads her mother's letters, and also "listens" to a poem spoken by her mother.

Laurel's memory is stirred once again by a written document: in one of her grandmother's letters addressed to her mother she finds a reference to herself as a little girl. Her grandmother mentions one of her pigeons, which she would like to send Laurel for her birthday. The pigeons and their typical way of regurgitating and feeding the already swallowed food to other pigeons evoked a feeling of terror and disgust when Laurel once observed this procedure at her grandmother's home:

> But Laurel had kept the pigeons under eye in their pigeon house and had already seen a pair of them sticking their beaks down each other's throats, gagging each other, eating out of each other's craws, swallowing down all over again what had been swallowed before: they were taking turns. The first time, she hoped they might never do it again, but they did it again next day while the other pigeons copied them. They convinced her that they could not escape each other and could not themselves be escaped. (p. 140)

This description is considered to be a key passage by some critics[47] because it reflects human needs and the difficulty in being dependent on each other. In connection with the grandmother's letter Louise Westling remarks that "the grandmother understands her granddaughter's fastidiousness about human commitments and wishes to involve her in the grotesque give-and-take of close human involvement illustrated by the pigeons' feeding off each other."[48] Laurel's intense reaction resembles Laura's when she is pushed into the water by her cousin and confronted with a knowledge that frightens her. Both girls undergo a kind of initiation rite that threatens their innocent minds. On a narratological level, the image of the pigeons with its implication of the cycle, indicated both by the regurgitation and the feeding of the young, also emphasizes the matrilinear narrative line. This aspect of matrilineage is further reinforced by the association of the pigeon/dove with Aphrodite, goddess of fertility. She is often described as accompanied by doves (and sparrows).[49]

The letter with the implicit reference to the little girl's fear and repulsion is finally the catalyst for Laurel's awareness that she has never really faced her grief about her husband's early death. Her husband, Phil Hand,[50] who was killed in World War II, has hardly been mentioned before this crucial passage. Noticing a photograph of her and Phil on her father's desk, she dismisses her memories: "Her marriage had been of magical ease, of *ease*—of brevity and conclusion and all belonging to Chicago and not here" (p. 121).[51] Only now, confronted with her own, her mother's, her grandmother's, and her father's grief, is Laurel ready to heed her sorrowful feelings towards her dead husband: "Now all she had found had found her" (p. 154). Laurel recognizes that she has preserved Phil in her memory as something untouchable, "sealed away," but "now, by her own hands, the past had been raised up" (p. 154). She even dares to raise the fear-inspiring question about a possible end of their marriage—if Phil had lived—and face the idea of an imperfect marriage with its implied anxiety and worries. The storm raging outside accompanies the storm taking place inside her, and she virtually has a vision of her dead husband. Lily Briscoe's last words in *To the Lighthouse*, "I have had my vision," are equally true for Laurel.

After her epiphany Laurel has a dream in which she is riding over a bridge on a train together with her husband. Once again awake, she recalls her real trip with Phil, travelling from Chicago to Mount Salus. In her memory she visualizes the confluence of the two rivers, the Ohio and the Mississippi. Now, Laurel no longer clings to the impervious past but to memory, which "is the somnambulist" (p. 179) and through which "all that is remembered joins, and lives—the old and the young, the past and the present, the living and the dead" (*OWB*, p. 104). Similarly, Virgie Rainey recognizes that "all the opposites on earth were close together" (*GA*, p. 234).

The passage about the confluence of the two rivers is, as mentioned at the beginning of this chapter, crucial for Eudora Welty's concept of memory and time. Her decision to include this passage at the end of her autobiographical book emphasizes the significance of memory and time. The additional comment after the quotation in *One Writer's Beginnings* establishes the connection between memory and time explicitly and with specific reference to the writer's involvement: "My own [memory] is the treasure most dearly regarded by me, in my life and in my work as a writer. Here time, also, is subject to confluence" (*OWB*, p. 104). The moment of memory makes confluence possible, but memory also makes it pass again: it is not static, but changing and moving.

Laurel's attitude towards her father's second wife, Fay, whom she meets after the crucial night, is a proof of her newly acquired insight that memory is not bound to possessions but is free and liable to continuity. By leaving her mother's beloved breadboard, which Phil made, to Fay, who is a person of the future,[52] she frees herself from the past and its memorabilia because she has more than enough of it in her memory. The numerous moments of memory, mainly triggered by her mother's own past, now make such a vision come true. Her memories can still frighten her, but she will not be trapped; the bird caught in the house is similarly freed by Laurel herself.

Woman's time and woman's memory are presented as the main sources of genuine vision in *The Optimist's Daughter*. The mother is the focus for the daughter in order to look backwards. It is not coincidental that Eudora Welty writes about mother-daughter relationships. Ellen Moers mentions many women writers who write

> about the motherhood of their mothers or grandmothers, not, certainly, their own. Cather and Stein never married; Virginia Woolf remained childless by design. . . .
>
> They wrote of the power and grandeur of motherhood with an air of finality, as if what they were describing would never come again; as if there would never more be any mothers. . . . These are mothers who "make of the moment something permanent," as Lily

> Briscoe says of Mrs. Ramsay in *To the Lighthouse*: they are women who say "Life stand still here."[53]

Yet, Moers also points out that, especially with regard to Virginia Woolf, there is not only homage paid in these mother portraits, there are "resentment, envy, the pain of betrayal, the cry of protest"[54] and descriptions of boredom in drawing rooms, at long dining tables, or in practical housework. In his comparison between *The Optimist's Daughter* and *To the Lighthouse*, Michael Kreyling comes to a different conclusion:

> The events and images of the novel [*The Optimist's Daughter*] are simple, homemade, yet charged with the possibility of a miraculous richness, or the threat of tinny emptiness. These are the same kinds of mundane, daily events out of which Virginia Woolf produces miracles.[55]

Indeed, the "simple, homemade" events refer to a woman's sphere, but they can often be the reasons for great anger and frustration, besides being the sources of "power and grandeur" or "miracles."

For Laurel her mother's room, her secretary, and the letters represent realms from which she can draw power and comfort, but again faced with her mother's death she must also endure moments of great pain and anxiety.[56] Memory to her has become the means to grasp the essence of time, that is, to recognize that there is past *and* memory, and that the former "can never be awakened," whereas the latter is "vulnerable to the living moment" and therefore lives. As "an optimist's daughter" she had to turn to her mother's time in order to find genuine memory. The "creative pursuit of the past" has made her "re-vision"[57] a successful one.

The book, focusing on "remembrance of things past," is a contribution to the literature of matrilineage. Although this novel is not mentioned among the hundreds of examples of mother-daughter portraits collected in *The Lost Tradition: Mothers and Daughters in Literature*,[58] it certainly belongs to this lost tradition. Moreover, the portrait of the protagonist's mother undermines the father portrait with its implications of male heroism[59] because the father is just the opposite of a hero (which Laurel recognizes immediately). On the contrary, the mother is the one "who *might* have done that" (dare to stand up against a mob, p. 80). Laurel, as her mother's daughter, has rediscovered this (potential) strength by remembering and by naming this female past, this "women's time."

6

# Conclusion

The analysis of Welty's novels with respect to her use of narrative strategies has shown that we can indeed speak of "female narrative strategies." The narrative structure underlying all the novels examined reflects a specifically female view of the world.

The analysis of point of view in *Delta Wedding* illustrates that the exclusively female point of view frequently focuses on (patriarchal and inhibiting) norms and conventions ruling on the plantation of Shellmound. The female characters as focalizers do not take a rebellious attitude (as for example Virgie does in *The Golden Apples*), but the emphasis attributed to their focalization on such gender-related issues evokes a questioning of these norms and conventions. To question male-dominant mechanisms does not necessarily imply rebellion against them; this strategy is only a step towards establishing female dominance. Viewed within the chronological order of Welty's novels, *Delta Wedding* indicates that this kind of female power does not yet make for strong and autonomous female characters, but it definitely dominates the narrative structure of the novel. Laura, the child, whose perspective is crucial throughout the book, might become a "Virgielike" woman who will despise the confining options of marriage (Dabney, or Jinny Love) and narrow-mindedness of a small town environment and will independently search for self-fulfillment.

The use of the exclusively female point of view undermines the culture text because the internal visions and expectations of the female protagonists obviously contrast with their concrete options. The cultural—and patriarchal—norms and conventions dominant in southern plantation life in the twenties are thus questioned and criticized as confining for the female protagonists. They cannot escape those norms, but they take over narrative power within a fictional world in which, after all, the culture text seems to be no longer valid for them; patriarchal authority is decentered: it is not effective in the narrative realm anymore.

In *The Golden Apples*, with its main theme of the wanderer and artist, the many references to myths also focus thematically on the sex role system. Welty's particular use of the classical myths and of the poems by Yeats is revealing with regard to her female characters: the presentation of these characters refutes the old, male-dominant story. By presenting the female characters both as victims (e.g., Snowdie MacLain, Mattie Will, or Easter) and as "heroines," the questioning of the sex role system is not a simple reversal of these roles, but vividly demonstrates their fundamental mechanisms (e.g., "Moon Lake"). Virgie, the heroine of the book, is the female wanderer who manages to pursue her search without being impeded by norms and conventions. She is not a real virgin, as her name suggests, but she is a virgin in the sense that she remains untouched by male hegemony.

The search for heroic fulfillment is presented within the traditional mythological context, which is male, but it is rewritten according to and for a female hero. The male heroic story is deconstructed (e.g., Loch's story in "Moon Lake") and replaced by a female vision of heroic longing and wandering. Moreover, the literary topos of the wandering artist emphasized by the allusion to Yeats's "Wandering Aengus" is used for the female protagonist: Virgie embodies both the wanderer and the artist searching for heroic fulfillment. Her vision of a heroic act with the implication of triumph *and* destruction, that is, considering hero and victim (Perseus/Medusa), does not encompass the only result (the deed) but also the necessary (re)creative dimension of human longing and suffering.

The speech behavior of Julia Mortimer and Gloria Renfro in *Losing Battles* contrasts strikingly with that of the many other clan members, who occupy most of the (reading) space in the book with their tales. The conscious and powerful use of language by the two female protagonists is not measurable by space but by influence on the community. Although they are outsiders (Julia the unmarried teacher, Gloria the orphan) like Laura and Virgie, they manage to defend themselves against the community. Julia, the teacher, is the most eminent fighter of battles against the community's conventional forces. Her weapon is the (written) word used in a reflective and critical way. After her death, her word is still heard and heeded: her voice in the narrative overcomes her own death.

The two female protagonists exercise authority dependent on their particular use of voice and/or silence. Their speech acts have much more (perlocutionary) force than the speech acts of the clan. Voice and silence of the female protagonists are effective weapons in the "losing battles" of the Banner community after all. Eudora Welty empowers them to speak in a language marked by the female gender.

In *The Optimist's Daughter*, Welty's last novel, the matriarchal world found in *Delta Wedding* takes an even more radical turn: the exploration of the female protagonist's past with regard to her dead parents is strongly influenced by the relationship with her mother and dominates her memories. Through Laurel's specific memory the narrative line becomes matrilinear. The death of the father does not coincide with the death of the narrative, as Roland Barthes posits:

> Death of the father would deprive literature of many of its pleasures. If there is no longer a father, why tell stories? Doesn't every narrative lead back to Oedipus? Isn't story-telling always a way of searching for one's origin, speaking one's conflict with the Law, entering into the dialectic of tenderness and hatred?[1]

Indeed, with the actual death of the father, Laurel begins to face the relationship with her mother and, finally, her own marriage. The search for her origin is triggered by her father's death. By exploring that past definitely closer to her, namely the past with her mother, Laurel can free herself from idealizing the past and be ready to confront the future. The exploration of the mother-daughter relationship makes evident that, even alive, the father has not had as much power and influence as the culture text makes us believe. With the focus on the mother, the position of the father is weakened, and the power of the mother-daughter bond is revealed: as in the other novels, patriarchal power is gradually taken over by the women, and a novel of matrilineage is created. The novel ends with Laurel's departure from her parental home. As for Virgie, and indeed for numerous other female characters in fiction by women writers, leaving is essential for a woman's search for self-fulfillment. The search proper lies in the future; her story can be a design for the future.

Eudora Welty, commenting on her relation to Virgie, the archetypal female wanderer and hero, emphasizes the crucial function Virgie has in her work: "Inasmuch as Miss Eckhart might have been said to come from me, the author, Virgie, at her moments, might have always been my subject" (*OWB*, p. 102). Welty, as a woman writer, gives multiple meanings to the "empty space" by focusing on such "subjects" as Virgie and by devising narrative strategies engendered by them.

# Notes

## CHAPTER 1

1. See the following articles in *Eudora Welty: Critical Essays*, ed. Peggy Whitman Prenshaw (Jackson, Miss.: University of Missisipi Press, 1979): Margaret Bolsterli, "Woman's Vision: The World of Women in *Delta Wedding*, *Losing Battles*, and *The Optimist's Daughter*," pp. 149–156; Julia L. Demmin and Daniel Curley, "The Golden Apples and the Silver Apples," pp. 242–257; Elizabeth Kerr, "The World of Eudora Welty's Women," pp. 132–148. See also Peggy Prenshaw, "Woman's World, Man's Place: The Fiction of Eudora Welty," in *Eudora Welty: A Form of Thanks*, ed. Louis Dollarhide and Ann J. Abadie (Jackson, Miss.: University Press of Mississippi, 1979), pp. 46–77; Louise Westling, *Sacred Groves and Ravaged Gardens: The Fiction of Eudora Welty, Carson McCullers, and Flannery O'Connor* (Athens, Ga.: University of Georgia Press, 1985); Patricia Yaeger, " 'Because a Fire Was in My Head': Eudora Welty and the Dialogic Imagination," *PMLA* 99, No. 5 (October 1984), 955–973 and "The Case of the Dan-

gling Signifier: Phallic Imagery in Eudora Welty's 'Moon Lake,' " *Twentieth Century Literature* 28, No. 4 (Winter 1982), 431–452.

2. The most important longer studies on this subject are: Louis Rubin, *Writers of the Modern South: The Faraway Country* (Seattle and London: University of Washington Press, 1963); Albert J. Devlin, *Eudora Welty's Chronicle: A Story of Mississippi Life* (Jackson, Miss.: University Press of Mississippi, 1983); Carol S. Manning, *With Ears Opening Like Morning Glories: Eudora Welty and the Love of Storytelling* (Westport, Conn., and London: Greenwood Press, 1985).

3. I use the French term, coined by the French feminist Hélène Cixous. The term does not designate something fixed, but rather contains a Utopian element in the sense that it refers to a future writing by women, which is not repressed by patriarchal language. See also Elaine Showalter, "Feminist Criticism in the Wilderness," in *Writing and Sexual Difference*, ed. Elizabeth Abel (Chicago: University of Chicago Press, 1982), p. 16.

4. Alice Walker, "Eudora Welty: An Interview," Summer 1973, in *Conversations with Eudora Welty*, ed. Peggy Prenshaw (Jackson, Miss.: University Press of Mississippi, 1984), pp. 135–136.

5. Barbaralee Diamonstein, "Eudora Welty," in ibid., p. 36; also Martha van Noppen, "A Conversation with Eudora Welty," in ibid., p. 250.

6. Virginia Woolf, *Women and Writing*, selected and introduced by Michèle Barrett (London: The Women's Press, 1979), p. 48.

7. Annette Kolodny, "Dancing through the Minefield: Some Observations on the Theory, Practice, and Politics of a Feminist Literary Criticism," *Feminist Studies* 6, No. 1 (Spring 1980), 18.

8. The term "muted group" is used by Edwin Ardener in his essay "The 'Problem' Revisited," in *Perceiving Women*, ed. Shirley Ardener (New York: Halsted Press, 1975), pp. 19–27.

9. Gerda Lerner, *The Majority Finds Its Past* (Oxford: Oxford University Press, 1979), p. 52.

10. See Ardener, "The 'Problem' Revisited," pp. 22–23.

11. See also Rachel Blau DuPlessis, *Writing beyond the Ending: Narrative Strategies of Twentieth-Century Women Writers* (Bloomington, Ind.: Indiana University Press, 1985), pp. 41–42, where DuPlessis also comments on Ardener's model.

12. Showalter, "Feminist Criticism in the Wilderness," p. 29.

13. Ardener, "The 'Problem' Revisited," p. 23.

14. Claudine Herrmann, "Les coordonnées féminines: espace et temps," in *Les voleuses de langue* (Paris: des femmes, 1976). The quotation is from the extract in *New French Feminisms*, ed. Elaine Marks and Isabelle de Courtivron (New York: Schocken Books, 1981), p. 169.

15. Ibid.

16. Hélène Cixous, "The Laugh of the Medusa," in Marks and de Courtivron, *New French Feminisms*, p. 255.

17. Sandra Gilbert and Susan Gubar, *The Madwoman in the Attic: The Woman Writer and the Nineteenth-Century Literary Imagination* (New Haven, Conn.: Yale University Press, 1979).

18. Susan Sniader Lanser and Evelyn Torton Beck use this term in their essay "[Why] Are There No Great Women Critics? And What Difference Does It Make?" in *The Prism of Sex: Essays in the Sociology of Knowledge*, ed. Julia A. Sherman and Evelyn Torton Beck (Madison: University of Wisconsin Press, 1979), p. 86. The use of this term has nothing to do with the "double-voiced" discourse used by Bakhtin and Vološinov. For them, "double-voiced" means the discourse of characters and nonauthorial narrators. See Susan Sniader Lanser, *The Narrative Act: Point of View in Prose Fiction* (Princeton, N.J.: Princeton University Press, 1981), pp. 47-48.

19. Rachel Blau DuPlessis mentions W.E.B. DuBois, who used this term to describe a black person's experience in a white society. See DuPlessis, *Writing beyond the Ending*, p. 42, and her note no. 42, p. 208.

20. Gertrude Stein, *Bee Time Vine. And Other Pieces (1913–1927)* (New Haven, Conn.: Yale University Press, 1953), pp. 254–294. See, for example, phrases such as "Patriarchal Poetry might be finished tomorrow" (p. 294).

21. See Patricia Meyer Spacks, *The Female Imagination* (New York: Avon Books, 1974), p. 4.

22. DuPlessis uses these expressions for the title of one of her chapters in *Writing beyond the Ending*. Virginia Woolf created them talking about Mary Carmichael in *A Room of One's Own* (London: The Hogarth Press, 1954): "First she broke the sentence; now she has broken the sequence" (p. 122).

23. Virginia Woolf, *Women and Writing*, p. 48.

24. I shall not give an overview of the achievements of feminist literary criticism. For a survey consult, for example, Showalter,

"Feminist Criticism in the Wilderness;" Josephine Donovan, *Feminist Literary Criticism: Explorations in Theory* (Lexington, Ky.: University Press of Kentucky, 1975); or K. K. Ruthven, *Feminist Literary Studies: An Introduction* (Cambridge, et al.: Cambridge University Press, 1984).

25. Annis Pratt, *Archetypal Patterns in Women's Fiction* (Bloomington, Ind.: Indiana University Press, 1981), or Carol Pearson and Katherine Pope, *The Female Hero in American and British Literature* (New York and London: R. R. Bowker, 1981).

26. See, for example, *The Voyage In: Fictions of Female Development*, ed. Elizabeth Abel, Marianne Hirsch, and Elizabeth Langland (Hanover and London: University Press of New England, 1983).

27. See DuPlessis, *Writing beyond the Ending*.

28. Showalter, "Feminist Criticism in the Wilderness," p. 13.

29. It is not the aim of this study to survey these approaches; I shall only give a few examples of the methods applied. Pychoanalysis: various essays in *The Future of Difference*, ed. Hester Eisenstein and Alice Jardine (New Brunswick, N.J.: Rutgers University Press, 1985); myth criticism: Annis Pratt, *Archetypal Patterns*; formalism, structuralism, and deconstruction: Mary Jacobus, *Women Writing and Writing about Women* (Totowa, N.J.: Barnes, 1979), or Patricia Yaeger, "Because a Fire" and "Dangling Signifier."

30. Rubin, *Writers of the Modern South*, p. 133.

31. Ibid. "Like the hummingbirds that appear frequently in her stories, it [her style] darts here and there, never quite coming to rest, tirelessly invoking light, color, the variety of experience" (pp. 133–134).

32. Ibid., p. 134.

33. Prenshaw, "Woman's World, Man's Place," pp. 46–77.

34. Ibid., p. 74.

35. Ibid., pp. 71–72.

36. Demmin and Curley, "Golden Apples and Silver Apples," p. 244.

37. There are two more essays on this subject in Prenshaw's anthology, but their emphasis is on a thematic study of the female characters in Welty's fiction. See Kerr, "World of Welty's Women," and Bolsterli, "Women's Vision."

38. See Yaeger, "Because a Fire" and "Dangling Signifier."

39. Westling, *Sacred Groves and Ravaged Gardens*, p. 68. Westling's most recent book on Welty, *Eudora Welty* (Basingstoke and London: Macmillan, 1989), was published just after this book went to press.

40. Anne Goodwyn Jones, *Tomorrow Is Another Day: The Woman Writer in the South, 1859–1936* (Baton Rouge and London: Louisiana State University Press, 1981). The writers are: Augusta Jane Evans, Grace King, Kate Chopin, Mary Johnston, Ellen Glasgow, Frances Newman, and Margaret Mitchell. For a more historical survey see Anne Firor Scott, *The Southern Lady: From Pedestal to Politics, 1830–1930* (Chicago: University of Chicago Press, 1970). Westling in her first chapter also gives an informative survey of southern women. See "The Blight of Southern Womanhood," in *Sacred Groves and Ravaged Gardens*, pp. 8–35.

41. Jones, *Tomorrow Is Another Day*, p. 41.

42. Ibid., p. 44. Jones uses Gilbert and Gubar's term from their book *The Madwoman in the Attic*.

43. See Jones, *Tomorrow Is Another Day*, p. 45.

44. Interestingly enough, Eudora Welty has said in an interview that she does not "mind being called a regional writer," in Linda Kuehl, "The Art of Fiction XLVII: Eudora Welty" (1972) in Prenshaw, *Conversations*, p. 87.

45. Chester Eisinger, "Traditionalism and Modernism in Eudora Welty," in *Eudora Welty: Thirteen Essays*, ed. Peggy Prenshaw (Jackson, Miss.: University Press of Mississippi, 1983), p. 4.

46. Ibid., pp. 6–7. The quotation by Welty is from *The Eye of the Story: Selected Essays and Reviews* (New York: Random House, 1978), pp. 114–115.

47. Eisinger, "Traditionalism and Modernism," p. 3. I shall return to Woolf's influence on Welty in the chapters on *Delta Wedding* and *The Optimist's Daughter*.

48. Judith Kegan Gardiner, "On Female Identity and Writing by Women," in Abel, *Writing and Sexual Difference*, p. 185.

49. Jonathan Culler, *The Pursuit of Signs* (London and Henley: Routledge & Kegan Paul, 1981), p. 50.

50. Ibid., pp. 169–170.

51. Lanser, *The Narrative Act*.

52. *The Golden Apples* is sometimes dealt with as a series of short stories. It is also included in *The Collected Stories of Eudora*

*Welty* (New York and London: Harcourt Brace Jovanovich, 1980). I definitely consider it as a novel since it is a homogeneous whole with character developments.

53. Christa Wolf, *Kassandra. Erzaehlung* (Darmstadt: Luchterhand, 1983).

54. My English translation of Christa Wolf, *Voraussetzungen einer Erzaehlung: Kassandra*, Frankfurter Poetik-Vorlesungen (Darmstadt: Luchterhand, 1983), p. 115.

55. "Circe," in *The Bride of the Innisfallen and Other Stories* (New York: Harcourt Brace Jovanovich, 1955), p. 110.

56. Margaret Atwood, "Circe/Mud Poems," in *You Are Happy* (New York: Harper & Row, 1974), pp. 46–70. Talking about myths in works by women writers, DuPlessis also mentions these poems. See DuPlessis, *Writing beyond the Ending*, pp. 110–112.

57. Ibid., p. 68.

58. Alicia Suskin Ostriker, *Stealing the Language: The Emergence of Women's Poetry in America* (Boston: Beacon Press, 1986), p. 212.

59. Adrienne Rich, "When We Dead Awaken: Writing as Re-Vision," in *On Lies, Secrets & Silence: Selected Prose 1966–1978* (New York: W. W. Norton, 1979), p. 35.

## CHAPTER 2

1. Prenshaw, "Woman's World, Man's Place," p. 54. It is interesting to note that in an interview Eudora Welty states that "[i]n the Delta it's very much of a matriarchy, especially in those years in the twenties that I was writing about, and really ever since the Civil War when the men were all gone and the women began to take over everything" (Prenshaw, *Conversations*, p. 304). Yet, one must not forget that the hegemony of the men continued all the same, even if white women had some authority on the plantations.

2. See also Jones, *Tomorrow Is Another Day*, pp. 9–11.

3. Prenshaw, "Woman's World, Man's Place," p. 48.

4. Diana Trilling, *The Nation* (May 11, 1946), p. 578.

5. Eudora Welty, *Delta Wedding* (New York: Harcourt Brace, 1946), p. 10. All page references in the text refer to this edition.

6. Trilling, *The Nation*, p. 578.

7. Lanser, *The Narrative Act*. All page references are given in the text.

8. For a definition of ideology, see ibid., p. 16. She refers to the original meaning of point of view given in the dictionary: "1. The position from which something is observed or considered; standpoint. 2. One's manner of viewing things; attitude." She explains that the second meaning implies a "point of view as an attitude or ideology by which one perceives or evaluates" (p. 16). In her opinion literary theorists should define point of view in terms of both technique and ideology, thus considering the two meanings given in the dictionary.

9. Lanser's concept of narrative stance concentrates on "the relationship between the narrator's personality and values and a 'culture text' or set of social and cultural norms against which literary discourse is conventionally read" (*The Narrative Act*, p. 184). The relationship between ideological stance and the culture text can be indicated by two axes: the axis of coincidence and that of significance. The axis of coincidence illustrates whether the narrator's ideological stance coincides with the culture text of the sending and/or receiving groups. Lanser aptly points out that a text may both contradict and corroborate both. *The Golden Apples* is an example that presents both cases.

10. Douglas Messerli, "The Problem of Time in Welty's *Delta Wedding*," *Studies in American Fiction* 5 (Fall 1977), 228.

11. In the chapter on *The Optimist's Daughter* the concept of time is more crucial for my approach to this particular novel; therefore, I shall elaborate on it in more detail in Chapter 4.

12. Eudora Welty, *The Optimist's Daughter* (New York: Harcourt Brace Jovanovich, 1972).

13. See also Messerli, "Problem of Time," 228.

14. Lucinda McKethan uses both "onlooker" and "seer" for Laura. See *The Dream of Arcady: Place and Time in Southern Fiction* (Baton Rouge and London: Louisiana State University Press, 1980), pp. 184, 188.

15. Examples are Hawthorne's Robin, Twain's Huck Finn, or Faulkner's Ike McCaslin. With respect to Robin in "My Kinsman, Major Molineux," Daniel G. Hoffman refers to the Freudian model of the search for the father in *Form and Fable in American Fiction* (New York: Oxford University Press, 1961), pp. 116–118. It is significant that for the girl Laura the search for the mother plays an essential role.

16. A similar episode reflecting the mysterious and at the same

time cruel belief can be found in George Eliot's novel *The Mill on the Floss*: Maggie Tulliver is deeply struck by a description in a book about a witch who must undergo the abominable test: if she swims she is a witch, if she drowns she is a good woman (London: Everyman's Library, 1977, p. 13).

17. James Joyce, *Ulysses* (London: The Bodley Head, 1960), p. 46 ("Gaze in your omphalos," ibid.).

18. "The Delta Cousins," typescript (Jackson, Miss.: Department of Archives and History), p. 26. See also Michael Kreyling, who mentions the sexual dimension in "The Delta Cousins," *Eudora Welty's Achievement of Order* (Baton Rouge and London: Louisiana State University Press, 1980), pp. 58–59.

19. In the chapter "Moon Lake" of *The Golden Apples*, Loch's rescue of Easter also conveys this aggressiveness towards the female. This episode will be dealt with in detail in the chapter on *The Golden Apples*. In the description of Loch's rescuing action we also find the phrase connoting fragmentation: "She was arm to arm and leg to leg in a long fold . . . " (*GA*, p. 128).

20. Louise Westling points out that in Woolf's *To the Lighthouse* Minta Doyle also loses a brooch; significantly, this happens when Paul Rayley proposes marriage to her. See Westling, *Sacred Groves and Ravaged Gardens*, p. 74.

21. Westling speaks of baptism in connection with this episode. Ibid., p. 91.

22. Peggy Prenshaw, "Cultural Patterns in Eudora Welty's *Delta Wedding* and 'The Demonstrators,' " *Notes on Mississippi Writers* 3 (Fall 1970), 53.

23. Eliot, *The Mill on the Floss*, pp. 280–281.

24. Kate Chopin, *The Awakening* (London: The Women's Press, 1978), pp. 189–190. Virgie in *The Golden Apples* also bathes in the river completely naked.

25. Ellen Moers, *Literary Women* (London: The Women's Press, 1978), p. 261.

26. For more detailed information on the name of Shellmound see Westling, *Sacred Groves and Ravaged Gardens*, p. 72, or Kreyling, *Achievement of Order*, p. 61.

27. John Edward Hardy, "*Delta Wedding* as Region and Symbol," *Sewanee Review* 60 (Summer 1952), 406.

28. Ibid.

29. "Narratee" is the translation of French "narrataire," denot-

ing Wolfgang Iser's "implied reader." See Lanser, *The Narrative Act*, p. 53.

30. In the section "Narrator and Male Characters" I shall recur to Battle's character.

31. See also Westling, *Sacred Groves and Ravaged Gardens*, p. 95.

32. Dorrit Cohn, *Transparent Minds: Narrative Modes for Presenting Consciousness in Fiction* (Princeton, N.J.: Princeton University Press, 1978), p. 126.

33. Tony Tanner, *The Reign of Wonder, Naivety and Reality in American Literature* (Cambridge: Cambridge University Press, 1965), p. 215.

34. Elisabeth Gruenewald-Huber, *Virginia Woolf: The Waves*, Swiss Studies in English 99 (Bern: Francke, 1979), pp. 98–99.

35. *The Eye of the Story*, p. 120.

36. Heide Seele and Chester E. Eisinger interpret Dabney's breaking of the night-light as a break with the past and her family. See Heide Seele, *Eudora Weltys "The Optimist's Daughter": ein Roman der Ambiguitaet* (Ph.D. diss., University of Heidelberg, Heidelberg, 1975), p. 118, and Chester E. Eisinger, *Fiction of the Forties* (Chicago: University of Chicago Press, 1963), p. 277.

37. Barbara MacKenzie, "The Eye of Time: The Photographs of Eudora Welty," in Prenshaw, *Critical Essays*, pp. 396–397.

38. Hardy, "*Delta Wedding* as Region and Symbol," 416.

39. Messerli, "Problem of Time," 233.

40. Robert Penn Warren, "The Love and The Separateness in Miss Welty," *Kenyon Review* 6 (Spring 1944), 249–250.

41. Kreyling also points out that "the very act of writing, when the clan's official medium of communication is oral, sets Shelley apart" (*Achievement of Order*, p. 69).

42. In "Moon Lake" in *The Golden Apples* Nina and Jinny Love also express their wish never to get married. See my section on "Moon Lake."

43. For a discussion of the role of the mother see my chapter on *The Optimist's Daughter*, in which I concentrate on the mother-daughter relationship.

44. Schoolteachers play an important role in Welty's work. Examples are Miss Eckhart (*GA*), Julia Mortimer (*LB*), and Becky McKelva (*OD*). In the respective chapters I deal with these characters in detail.

45. *The Eye of the Story*, p. 165.

46. In the short story "A Still Moment," the fusion of stillness, beauty, and art is the main theme.

47. Moers, *Literary Women*, p. 236.

48. See also Westling, *Sacred Groves and Ravaged Gardens*, p. 73.

49. Devlin, *Eudora Welty's Chronicle*, p. 120.

50. Ruth M. Vande Kieft, *Eudora Welty* (New York: Twayne, 1962), p. 108.

51. Trilling, *The Nation*, p. 578.

52. Cf. also Madelon Sprengnether, "*Delta Wedding* and the Kore Complex," *Southern Quarterly* 25, No. 2 (Winter 1987), 122.

53. Elizabeth Abel, "Narrative Structure(s) and Female Development: The Case of *Mrs. Dalloway*," in *The Voyage In: Fictions of Female Development*, ed. Elizabeth Abel, Marianne Hirsch, and Elizabeth Langland (Hanover and London: University Press of New England, 1983), p. 163.

54. Vande Kieft, *Eudora Welty*, p. 95.

55. Lanser, *The Narrative Act*, pp. 141–142.

## CHAPTER 3

1. Harry C. Morris, "Eudora Welty's Use of Mythology," *Shenandoah* 6 (Spring 1955), 34.

2. Ibid.

3. Ibid., 40.

4. Thomas L. McHaney, "Eudora Welty and the Multitudinous Apples," *Mississippi Quarterly* 26, No. 4 (Fall 1973), 598–624. McHaney's article in the special Eudora Welty issue of *Mississippi Quarterly* is one of the most informative and extensive studies on the use of myths in *The Golden Apples*. McHaney deals with both the Celtic and Graeco-Roman mythologies recurred to by Welty.

5. Danièle Pitavy-Souques, "Technique as Myth: The Structure of *The Golden Apples*," in Prenshaw, *Critical Essays*, pp. 258–268. See also Robert L. Phillips's article in the same book: "A Structural Approach to Myth in the Fiction of Eudora Welty," pp. 56–67.

6. T. S. Eliot in his review of *Ulysses* in *The Dial* (1923).

7. As mentioned above, *The Golden Apples* is dealt with both as a series of short stories and as a novel in criticism.

8. Pitavy-Souques, "Technique as Myth," p. 262.

9. See for example *Intertextuality in Faulkner*, ed. Michel Gresset and Noel Polk (Jackson, Miss.: University of Mississippi Press, 1985).

10. Patricia Yaeger, " 'Because a Fire.' " I am especially indebted to this article because of its specific references to the two poems by Yeats.

11. Ibid., 955. The second quote is from Bakhtin, "From the Prehistory of Novelistic Discourse," *The Dialogic Imagination*, trans. Caryl Emerson and Michael Holquist (Austin: University of Texas Press, 1981), p. 294.

12. Ibid., 970.

13. See the term "transsexuation," which Genette uses in his *Palimpsestes. La littérature au second degré* (Paris: Seuil, 1982), p. 436, note 2.

14. See Yaeger, " 'Because a Fire,' " 969.

15. *The Golden Apples* (New York: Harcourt Brace, 1947), p. 85. All page references in the text refer to this edition.

16. W. B. Yeats, *The Collected Poems of W. B. Yeats* (London: Macmillan & Co., 1961), p. 66.

17. Ibid., p. 241.

18. Ibid.

19. See Jonathan Culler on Lévi-Strauss in *Structuralist Poetics* (Ithaca, N.Y.: Cornell University Press, 1976), pp. 40–41.

20. See Robert Scholes, *Structuralism in Literature* (New Haven, Conn., and London: Yale University Press, 1974), p. 69.

21. See notes 8 and 9 of my introduction.

22. It is interesting to note that this guitar player has female traits and almost appears as an androgynous character. See my section on "Music in Spain."

23. Yaeger states that "King becomes both 'muse' and narrative subject in the fables the women of Morgana tell themselves" (Yaeger, " 'Because a Fire,' " 960).

24. To swan, v. [1]: to swim like a swan. v [2]: U.S. slang, probably northern English dialect "Is' wan" (I shall warrant = I'll be bound. Later taken as a mincing substitute for swear) (*OED*, vol. XVII, 2nd ed., ed. James A. H. Murray et al. Prepared by J. A. Simpson and E.S.C. Weiner [London: Clarendon Press, 1989]).

25. For an interpretation of this passage see my section on "The Wanderers."

26. Yaeger, " 'Because a Fire,' " 963.

27. Vande Kieft, *Eudora Welty*, p. 118.

28. Looking at the single women in the novels by Ellen Glasgow (*The Barren Ground*) or Willa Cather (*My Ántonia, O Pioneers!*), one notices that these women are much stronger characters than those in Welty's novels. Moreover, they are more closely tied to the land.

29. Elaine Upton Pugh also mentions Cassie's capacity to see and perceive her surroundings in a way that brings them closer to the reader. See "The Duality of Morgana: The Making of Virgie's Vision, the Vision of *The Golden Apples*," *Modern Fiction Studies* 28, No. 3 (Fall 1982), 438. I do not quite agree with Danièle Pitavy-Souques, whose article "Watchers and Watching: Point of View in Eudora Welty's 'June Recital,' " *Southern Review* 19 (January 1983), 483–509, stresses the importance and equality of Loch's and Cassie's points of view.

30. "Shillelagh": Irish for "cudgel." Reference to Yeats's Irish nationality.

31. Geoffrey Hartman, *Criticism in the Wilderness* (New Haven, Conn., and London: Yale University Press, 1980), p. 23.

32. Yaeger, " 'Because a Fire,' " 961. In her revised article in *Mississippi Quarterly* 39, No. 4 (Fall 1986), special Eudora Welty issue, Yaeger comments on readers who, like myself, do not take Mattie Will's encounter with King for a fantasy, " 'Because a Fire,' " 569.

33. Hartman, *Criticism in the Wilderness*, p.23

34. Yaeger, "Dangling Signifier," 431.

35. Ibid. See also DuPlessis on "displacement," *Writing beyond the Ending*, p. 108, and her note 10, p. 226.

36. See also Yaeger, "Dangling Signifier," 440–441.

37. Rubin, *Writers of the Modern South*, p. 148.

38. Yaeger, "Dangling Signifier," 449.

39. Annie Leclerc, from *Parole de Femme* (Paris: Grasset, 1974) in *New French Feminisms*, p. 79.

40. Mary Anne Ferguson, "The Female Novel of Development and the Myth of Psyche," in Abel et al., *The Voyage In*, p. 234.

41. Ibid., p. 232.

42. Kreyling, *Achievement of Order*, p. 93.

43. Yeats, *Collected Poems*, p. 101.

44. McHaney, "Eudora Welty and the Multitudinous Apples," 609–610.

45. Richard Ellman, *The Identity of Yeats* (London: Faber and Faber, 1954), p. 112.

46. McHaney, "Eudora Welty and the Multitudinous Apples," 610.

47. McHaney, among others, mentions the parallel to the Perseus story: Perseus cuts off Medusa's head and then goes to the west of the earth. Furthermore, McHaney draws our attention to Miss Eckhart: she, too, slaps her mother across the face. Ibid., 600–601, 613.

48. Joyce, *Ulysses*, pp. 85–107. See also Devlin, *Eudora Welty's Chronicle*, p. 204.

49. McHaney, "Eudora Welty and the Multitudinous Apples," 612.

50. Vande Kieft, *Eudora Welty*, p. 137.

51. McHaney, "Eudora Welty and the Multitudinous Apples," 617.

52. Chopin, *The Awakening*, p. 189.

53. Moers, *Literary Women*, p. 260. Jane Flax explains that "[i]t is significant that *Civilization and Its Discontents* begins with Freud discussing his inability to grasp a certain 'oceanic' feeling (about which Romain Roland had written him). This oceanic feeling seems to capture the affect of the early symbiotic unity between mother and child" ("Mother-Daughter Relationships: Psychodynamics, Politics, and Philosophy," in Eisenstein and Jardine, *The Future of Difference*, p. 26).

54. Moers, *Literary Women*, p. 261.

55. Moers mentions the specific names that women writers have given their landscapes, e.g., Black Valley, The Red Deeps, etc. (ibid., p. 255). Welty's Big Black River certainly suggests a sexual realm.

56. Pearson and Pope, *The Female Hero*, p. 63.

57. Ibid.

58. See also Pearson and Pope's comment on Anna, the female protagonist in Doris Lessing's *The Golden Notebook*; they state that "[t]he recognition that the dragon exists as both an external and internal force may occur in a visionary moment" (ibid., p. 64).

59. Kreyling, *Achievement of Order*, p. 105.

60. Vande Kieft, *Eudora Welty*, p. 142. See also Pugh, "The Duality of Morgana," 435–451. Jill Fritz-Piggott also comments on the dual nature of reality in *The Golden Apples*, in "The Sword and the Song: Moments of Intensity in *The Golden Apples*," *Southern Literary Journal* 18, No. 2 (Spring 1986), 30.

61. Sigmund Freud, *Drei Abhandlungen zur Sexualtheorie* (Frankfurt am Main: Fischer Taschenbuchverlag, 1961), p. 157.

62. Both Ostriker and DuPlessis mention May Sarton's poem "The Muse as Medusa" in *Selected Poems* (New York: W. W. Norton, 1978), pp. 155–166, when dealing with a re-vision of myth. See DuPlessis, *Writing beyond the Ending*, p. 109, and Ostriker, *Stealing the Language*, p. 215. It is striking how many women writers rely on the myth of Medusa. See for example also Elizabeth G. Gitter, "The Power of Women's Hair in the Victorian Imagination," *PMLA* 99, No. 5 (October 1984), 950. Gitter mentions Medusa in connection with Christina Rossetti's "Eden Bower." In *The Optimist's Daughter* there is also an allusion to the Medusa myth, but in my opinion it plays a minor role in this book. See Naoko Fuwa Thornton's essay "Medusa-Perseus Symbolism in Eudora Welty's *The Optimist's Daughter*," *The Southern Quarterly* 23, No. 4 (Summer 1985), 64–76.

63. John Allen also refers to this dual aspect. See John Allen, "Eudora Welty: The Three Moments" in *A Still Moment. Essays on the Art of Eudora Welty*, ed. John F. Desmond, (Metuchen, N.J., and London: The Scarecrow Press, 1978), p. 15.

64. In "Technique as Myth" Danièle Pitavy-Souques sees Perseus, Medusa, and the mirror shield as the three mythological elements in relation to the artist: "Welty's art becomes reflexive, just as literature, she seems to suggest, is a mirror. She questions her art in the very moment she is creating it. Somehow, those 'quotations' [from mythology] are the play within the play, contesting the story and the genre while functioning within it. They constitute the mirror that Welty holds to her fiction. Perseus does nothing else: the writer *is* Perseus" (Prenshaw, *Critical Essays*, p. 262). Pitavy-Souques refers to Reynolds Price's statement that "[t]he central myth of the artist is surely not Narcissus but Perseus—with the artist in all roles, Perseus, Medusa and the mirror-shield" (Reynolds Price, *Things Themselves* [New York: Atheneum, 1972], p. 8).

65. Iris Murdoch, *A Severed Head* (New York, 1966), p. 198.

66. Ibid.

67. Scholes, *Structuralism in Literature*, p. 197.

68. Ibid. Scholes comments on the relationship of structuralism to existentialism as follows: "Existential Marxism assumes that man is *in history*, moving toward a better future in a progressive way. Structuralism assumes that man is in a system not necessarily arranged for his benefit. Structuralism has accepted the main insights of modern science as existentialism has not" (p. 194).

69. Barbara Johnson, *The Critical Difference* (Baltimore and London: Johns Hopkins University Press, 1980), p. 13.

70. Scholes, *Structuralism in Literature*, pp. 198–199.

71. Louis D. Rubin, "Thomas Wolfe in Time and Place," in *Southern Renascence*, ed. Louis D. Rubin and Robert D. Jacobs (Baltimore: Johns Hopkins University Press, 1966), p. 292.

72. See also Pitavy-Souques, "Technique as Myth," in Prenshaw, *Critical Essays*, p. 261.

73. Demmin and Curley, "Golden Apples and Silver Apples," in Prenshaw, *Critical Essays*, p. 257.

74. The old beggar woman is called Minerva (cf. p. 238), and McHaney refers to ancient Minerva, who chose the old woman for one of her disguises. See McHaney, "Eudora Welty and the Multitudinous Apples," p. 620.

## CHAPTER 4

1. For a discussion of *Losing Battles* as a comic epic, see Mary Anne Ferguson, "*Losing Battles* as a Comic Epic in Prose," in Prenshaw, *Critical Essays*, pp. 305–324, and Carol S. Manning's chapter "*Losing Battles*: Tall Tale and Comic Epic," pp. 137–162. Both critics also mention the similarities between *Losing Battles* and the *Odyssey* (e.g., a hero who returns home).

2. Ferguson gives an informative survey of the first reactions after the publication of the novel (Ferguson, "*Losing Battles* as a Comic Epic in Prose," in Prenshaw, *Critical Essays*, pp. 305–306). See also Kreyling, *Achievement of Order*, pp. 140–142.

3. Robert Heilman, "Losing Battles and Winning the War," in Prenshaw, *Critical Essays*, p. 274.

4. Kuehl, "The Art of Fiction XLVII," in Prenshaw, *Conversations*, p. 77.

5. Ibid., p. 76.

6. Ibid., p. 77.

7. Seymour Chatman, "The Structure of Narrative Transmission," in *Style and Structure in Literature. Essays in the New Stylistics*, ed. Roger Fowler (Ithaca, N.Y.: Cornell University Press, 1975), p. 244.

8. Ibid., p. 230.

9. Kuehl, "The Art of Fiction XLVII," in Prenshaw, *Conversations*, p. 77.

10. *The Eye of the Story*, pp. 33, 35. Welty speaks of "the interior of our lives," p. 30.

11. Kuehl, "The Art of Fiction XLVII," in Prenshaw, *Conversations*, p. 77.

12. I exclude Jack, Gloria's husband, who is not a mere talker, because his speech behavior is not extraordinary at all compared to that of the two women. Moreover, he sometimes participates in the family's tale telling.

13. Elizabeth Evans, *Eudora Welty* (New York: Frederick Ungar, 1981), p. 83.

14. *Losing Battles* (New York: Random House, 1970), p. 432. All page references in the text are to this edition.

15. J. L. Austin, *How To Do Things with Words*, ed. J. O. Urmson and Marina Sbisà (Cambridge, Mass.: Harvard University Press, 1962), pp. 109–110.

16. Lanser, *The Narrative Act*, p. 284.

17. Mary Louise Pratt, *Toward a Speech Act Theory of Literary Discourse* (Bloomington, Ind.: Indiana University Press, 1977).

18. John R. Searle, *Expression and Meaning: Studies in the Theory of Speech Acts* (Cambridge: Cambridge University Press, 1979; rpt. 1986), p. 64.

19. Seymour Chatman, *Story and Discourse: Narrative Structure in Fiction and Film* (Ithaca, N.Y., and London: Cornell University Press, 1978), p. 165. See also Wolfgang Iser, "Die Wirklichkeit der Fiktion," in *Rezeptionsaesthetik*, ed. Rainer Warning (Munich: Wilhelm Fink Verlag, 1975), p. 288. Iser comments on the illocutionary force of fictional texts.

20. Richard Ohmann, "Literature as Act," in *Approaches to Poetics*, Selected Papers from the English Institute, ed. Seymour Chatman (New York and London: Columbia University Press, 1973). Ohmann provides us with an analysis of speech acts of characters, which is an evident illustration that illocutionary acts

can be attributed to fictional characters. Ohmann describes the speech acts of some characters in Shaw's play *Major Barbara*, concluding that "[i]llocutions are the vehicle of the play's action" because they "move the play along" (p. 89). These illocutionary acts consist of promising, welcoming, questioning, rating, conjecturing, etc. (cf. pp. 85–89). Ohmann does not mention any perlocutionary acts, although he states that Major Barbara resigns from the army as a consequence of what was said in the piece of dialogue analyzed by Ohmann. I would describe this effect of particular sentences on Major Barbara as a perlocutionary act.

21. Ibid., pp. 97–98.

22. Ohmann refers to the concept of "mimesis" in connection with the reader-writer relation: "Mimesis draws into play the reader's social self"(ibid., p. 99).

23. See Ohmann's example of the difference in reader participation of *Lady Chatterley's Lover*: "for most of the women students in my class last year the book was objectionable in a more immediate way. They said to participate in the mimetic re-creation of Connie Chatterley as Lawrence saw her was for them impossible without self-betrayal" (ibid., p. 106).

24. Louis Rubin, "Everything Brought Out into the Open: Eudora Welty's *Losing Battles*," in *William Elliott Shoots a Bear: Essays on the Southern Literary Imagination* (Baton Rouge: Louisiana University Press, 1975), p. 215.

25. See also Heilman, "Losing Battles and Winning the War," in Prenshaw, *Thirteen Essays*, pp. 178–179. Heilman enumerates some personal traits of the various characters, but he, too, states that "the individual psyche is not quite the business of the novel" (p. 179).

26. Kreyling, *Achievement of Order*, p. 148.

27. James Boatwright, "Speech and Silence in *Losing Battles*," *Shenandoah* 25, No. 3 (Spring 1974), 9.

28. Eliot, *Mill on the Floss*, pp. 139–140.

29. Prenshaw, "Woman's World, Man's Place: The Fiction of Eudora Welty" in Dollarhide and Abadie, *A Form of Thanks*, p. 68.

30. DuPlessis also mentions this characteristic of female protagonists. Yet, commenting on *Jane Eyre*, she points out that "[t]he critique of social conditions that orphans symbolize (poverty, vulnerability, exclusion) will be muted by the achievement of the blessed state of normalcy, so thrillingly different from depriva-

tion. Through the mechanism of orphans, novels can present standard family, kinship, and gender relations as if these were a utopian ideal" (*Writing beyond the Ending*, p. 9).

31. Manning points out that "[t]o Gloria, watermelon, which the otherwise barren land produces in bushel-basket size, is representative of Beechanism—common and low-class" ("Tall Tale and Comic Epic," p. 158).

32. Seymour Gross in Prenshaw, *Thirteen Essays*, p. 200. This statement reflects an attitude that uncritically assumes that a woman should not yearn for autonomy and independence.

33. See Kreyling, *Achievement of Order*, p. 148.

34. For Welty's use of parody in *Losing Battles*, see also Manning, "Tall Tale and Comic Epic," especially pp. 142–149.

35. See Evans, *Eudora Welty*, pp. 83–84, Heilman, "Losing Battles and Winning the War," in Prenshaw, *Thirteen Essays*, pp. 182–183, or Jennifer Lynn Randisi, *A Tissue of Lies: Eudora Welty and the Southern Romance* (Washington, D.C.: University Press of America, 1982), p. 99.

36. See Heilman, "Losing Battles and Winning the War," in Prenshaw, *Thirteen Essays*, p. 183. Heilman deals with the specific scenes which can be related to the biblical story. Heilman speaks of chivalric heroism in connection with Jack. He lists "honor" as one of the essential driving forces for Jack (p. 184.)

37. Ferguson, "*Losing Battles* as a Comic Epic," in Prenshaw, *Critical Essays*, p. 308. Ferguson quotes Hassan's statement, which describes "radical innocence" as "man's quenchless desire to affirm, despite the voids and vicissitudes of our age, the human sense of *life*!" See Ihab Hassan, *Radical Innocence: Studies in the Contemporary American Novel* (Princeton, N.J.: Princeton University Press, 1961), p. 6.

38. Ferguson, "*Losing Battles* as a Comic Epic," in Prenshaw, *Critical Essays*, p. 309.

39. Prenshaw in Dollarhide, *A Form of Thanks*, p. 66.

40. Judge Moody, to whom Julia Mortimer's letter is addressed, is, like Jack, an exception among the male talkers. As his title indicates, he is an intellectual who once was Julia's pupil. He stands in sharp contrast to the members of the reunion, and he is also one of the very few who take Julia's side; he is emotionally upset when he learns how Julia died.

41. See also Ferguson's comment on women in *Losing Battles*,

"*Losing Battles* as a Comic Epic," in Prenshaw, *Critical Essays*, pp. 322–323; I do not quite agree with her statement that (all) the women in the book have a "clear-eyed view." As I have shown, it is mainly Julia and Gloria who have "common sense" (*LB*, p. 140).

42. M. E. Bradford, "Looking Down from a High Place: The Serenity of Miss Welty's *Losing Battles*," in Desmond, *A Still Moment*, p. 109.

43. Julia Kristeva also uses this word in her essay "Women's Time," trans. Alice Jardine and Harry Blake, *Signs* 1 (Fall 1981), 30.

## CHAPTER 5

1. *One Writer's Beginnings* (Cambridge, Mass., and London: Harvard University Press, 1984). All page references in the text refer to this edition.

2. "Some Notes on Time in Fiction," in *The Eye of the Story*, p. 171. Originally published in the *Mississippi Quarterly* 26, No. 4 (Fall 1973), 483–492. For the quotation by Faulkner see *Light in August* (London: Chatto & Windus, 1960), p. 111.

3. Ibid.

4. Ibid., p. 169.

5. Vladimir Nabokov, *Ada, or Ardor: A Family Chronicle* (New York: McGraw-Hill, 1969), p. 559. Patricia Drechsel Tobin refers to this novel in her study *Time and the Novel: The Genealogical Imperative* (Princeton, N.J.: Princeton University Press, 1978). See Chapter 5, pp. 133–163.

6. Tobin, *Time and the Novel*, p. 5. Cf. also the emblematic presentation of time as a male figure with wings, for example, in *Pericles, Prince of Tyre* IV. Chorus 47, or *The Winter's Tale*, IV. 1. 4. Moreover, in Greek mythology Cronus is the male god who devoured his children. See also Ovid, *Metamorphoses*, XV, 234–235: "tempus edax rerum." In one of her poems, Adrienne Rich ironically refers to the male concept of time: "Sigh no more, ladies. / Time is male / and in his cups drinks to the fair." In "Snapshots of a Daughter-in-Law," in *Poems: Selected and New 1950–1974* (New York: W. W. Norton, 1975), p. 50.

7. Tobin, *Time and the Novel*, p. 12.

8. I rely on Tobin, who states that time in fictional narratives

is similar to real-life experience of time. She mentions philosophical explanations of the linearity of thought and language structure. See ibid., pp. 18–20.

9. Ibid., p. 163.

10. Kristeva, "Women's Time," 15–17. Kristeva does not give the reference to the Joyce quotation. After my painstaking search, Joyce scholar Fritz Senn finally informed me that the phrase is from *Finnegans Wake*, but not as Kristeva quotes it. The correct phrase goes: "Father Times and Mother Spacies"(*Finnegans Wake* [London: Faber and Faber, 1939], p. 600).

Interestingly enough, Kristeva refers to Cronus as he appears in Hesiod's mythology as an example of monumental temporality (p. 16). I see Cronus as a further example of the masculine principle of time: he devours his own children because he is afraid that they might usurp his power. With respect to Kristeva's emphasis on space as far as women are concerned, see also Pitavy-Souques's point in "Le Sud: territoire des femmes?" *Revue Française d'Etudes Américaines* 10 (February 1985), 38. Pitavy-Souques speaks of "spatialisation du temps" with regard to the cycle of the year mainly represented in *Losing Battles* through the moon, a tree, and the celebration.

11. Mary Daly, *Pure Lust: Elemental Feminist Philosophy* (London: The Women's Press, 1984), p. 172.

12. Ibid., p. 173. The quotation in the last sentence given by Daly is from Virginia Woolf, *Moments of Being*, ed. Jeanne Schulkind (New York: Harcourt Brace Jovanovich, 1976), p. 72.

13. Ibid. Commenting on female identity and writing, Judith Kegan Gardiner states that many women writers "feel that women remember what men choose to forget. If memory operates in the service of identity maintenance differently in the two sexes, it will appear differently in literature by women" ("On Female Identity and Writing by Women," in Abel, *Writing and Sexual Difference*, p. 188).

14. Kuehl, "The Art of Fiction XLVII," in Prenshaw, *Conversations*, p. 75. Eudora Welty emphasizes that she was especially fascinated by *To the Lighthouse* and reread the novel several times.

15. Cf. also Heinrich Straumann, *American Literature in the Twentieth Century* (London: Arrow Books, 1962), rev. ed., p. 163. Straumann mentions the similarity between Woolf and Welty (even before *The Optimist's Daughter* was published).

16. Kreyling, *Achievement of Order*, p. 153.

17. Abel, "Narrative Structure(s) and Female Development," in Abel et al., *The Voyage In*, p. 163.

18. *The Optimist's Daughter* (New York: Harcourt Brace Jovanovich, 1972), p. 4. All page numbers refer to this edition and are given in the text. A story with the same title was published in the *New Yorker* in 1969 (*New Yorker*, March 15). For a comparison between the story and the novel see Helen Hurt Tiegreen, "Mothers, Daughters, and One Writer's Revisions," *Mississippi Quarterly* 39, No. 4 (Fall 1986), special Eudora Welty issue, 605–626, or Kreyling, *Achievement of Order*, pp. 171–172.

19. It is interesting to note that for both memory and retina the verb "slipped" is used.

20. Although the fear of expressing "false hope" (p. 29) is explicitly stated by the third-person narrator and not by Laurel herself in either direct speech or indirect interior monologue, I read it as Laurel's own recognition because we mostly see through Laurel's eyes. Moreover, the conditional "it might be false hope" is closer to Laurel's wavering feelings.

21. Kreyling, *Achievement of Order*, p. 154.

22. In connection with Woolf's *To the Lighthouse* Kreyling also refers to the importance of seeing, "a light-house, for instance" (*Achievement of Order*, p. 155).

23. Flax, "Mother-Daughter Relationships" in Eisenstein and Jardine, *The Future of Difference* (Boston: G. K. Hall, 1980), p. 23.

24. For a definition of differentiation see Nancy Chodorow, "Gender, Relation, and Difference in Psychoanalytic Perspective," in ibid., pp. 5–6.

25. Flax criticizes Freud for not fully examining the pre-Oedipal period, which, as Flax explains, is crucial for the development of gender difference. See ibid., pp. 22–26.

26. In Woolf's novel, *Mrs. Dalloway*, the pre-Oedipal period also plays an important role. See Abel, "Narrative Structure(s) and Female Development," in Abel et al., *The Voyage In*, p. 164.

27. For detailed discussion of the bird imagery and especially of the chimney swift see Marilyn Arnold's article "Images of Memory in Eudora Welty's *The Optimist's Daughter*," *Southern Literary Journal* 14 (Spring 1982), 29–31, 34–37. Prenshaw states that Laurel "invites death into the house" ("Woman's World, Man's Place," in Dollarhide and Abadie, *A Form of Thanks*, p. 70).

28. See also Westling, *Sacred Groves and Ravaged Gardens*, p. 106.

29. In *One Writer's Beginnings* Welty speaks of her own mother as "that great keeper, my mother" (p. 75) who kept all the letters, including the ones written by her and sent to Welty's father. In the novel emphasis is laid on the fact that the father destroyed his letters.

30. *The Eye of the Story*, p. 163.

31. Ibid., pp. 163–164.

32. Welty continues to explain that "the novelist lives on closer terms with time than he does with place" (ibid., p. 164) because time determines the course of the novel (ibid., p. 167).

33. Ibid., p. 168.

34. Dealing with time in *The Optimist's Daughter*, Heide Seele also refers to McKelva's growing awareness of time in *Eudora Weltys "The Optimist's Daughter,"* p. 53.

35. Eudora Welty's own mother was from West Virginia. See *One Writer's Beginnings*, p. 50. For the specific influence of West Virginia in Welty's work, see Barbara Wilkie Tedford, "West Virginia Touches in Eudora Welty's Fiction," *Southern Literary Journal* 18, No. 2 (Spring 1986), 40–52.

36. Westling also quotes this passage as an example of a typically female landscape (*Sacred Groves and Ravaged Gardens*, p. 106). Westling refers to Ellen Moers's *Literary Women*, which lists such female landscapes by various women writers (Moers, *Literary Women*, pp. 254–264).

37. Although the name "Queen's Shoals" is a real name (cf. *OWB*, p. 54), I consider "Queen's Shoals" to be one of those names given by women writers that Moers regards as "sexually suggestive" (Moers, *Literary Women*, p. 255).

38. Ibid., p. 254.

39. According to Freud, trees, as well as sticks, umbrellas, etc., connote the male sexual organ (quoted by Moers, ibid., p. 252).

40. Ibid., p. 257.

41. *One Time, One Place* (New York: Random House, 1971), p. 8.

42. In a collection of poems exclusively on mother-daughter relationships, a great number of poems deals with the daughters' sorrows at the deaths of their mothers (Lynn Lifshin, *Tangled Vines: A Collection of Mother and Daughter Poems* [Boston: Beacon Press, 1978]). See especially the poems by Erica Jong ("Mother," pp. 49–

52), Honor Moore (from the play *Mourning Pictures*, p. 82), and Adrienne Rich ("A Woman Mourned by Daughters," pp. 83–84).

43. Martha van Noppen, "A Conversation with Eudora Welty," in Prenshaw, *Conversations*, pp. 241–242.

44. See Welty's memory of her own grandmother's letters to her mother, *One Writer's Beginnings*, pp. 55–56.

45. Welty comments on the differences between Miss Eckhart and Julia Mortimer: "Miss Eckhart was a very mysterious character. Julia Mortimer was much more straightforward and dedicated and thinking of the people as somebody she wanted to help. Miss Eckhart was a very strange person" (Jo Brans, "Struggling against the Plaid: An Interview with Eudora Welty," in Prenshaw, *Conversations*, p. 304). See also her comment on Miss Eckhart in *OWB*, p. 102.

46. Françoise Basch, *Relative Creatures. Victorian Women in Society and Novel 1837–67*, trans. A. Rudolf (London, 1974), p. 112.

47. Cf. Devlin, *Eudora Welty's Chronicle*, p. 180; Kreyling, *Achievement of Order*, p. 169; Westling, *Sacred Groves and Ravaged Gardens*, p. 107; Seele, *Eudora Weltys "The Optimist's Daughter,"* p. 119. Cf. also Welty's own comment in an interview, Martha van Noppen, *Conversations*, p. 241.

48. Westling, *Sacred Groves and Ravaged Gardens*, p. 107.

49. See Robert Graves, *The Greek Myths* (Harmondsworth, England: Penguin Books, 1955), vol. 1, pp. 49–50.

50. The name "Hand" emphasizes Phil's "large, good hands" (p. 161) and his talent at designing and making things.

51. This statement is put in parentheses (cf. p. 121); they enforce Laurel's tendency to shrug her feelings off with respect to her dead husband.

52. For a more detailed discussion of Fay, see for example Daniel Thomas Young, "Social Forms and Social Order: Eudora Welty's *The Optimist's Daughter*," in *The Past in the Present: A Thematic Study of Modern Southern Fiction* (Baton Rouge and London: Louisiana State University Press, 1981), pp. 87–115, Devlin, *Eudora Welty's Chronicle*, pp. 181–182, or MacKethan, *The Dream of Arcady*, pp. 203–204.

53. Moers, *Literary Women*, p. 236. Like Gertrude Stein or Willa Cather, Eudora Welty never married or had children. The reference to the quotation by Woolf is *To the Lighthouse* (Harmondsworth, England: Penguin Books, 1964), p. 183.

54. Ibid., p. 237.

55. Kreyling, *Achievement of Order*, p. 154.

56. See also Westling's comment that writing this novel "apparently gave her [Welty] a way of confronting her mother's death and accepting her grief, a process reflected in Laurel Hand's painful reassessment of her mother's character" (*Sacred Groves and Ravaged Gardens*, p. 45).

57. Adrienne Rich uses this term in her essay "When We Dead Awaken: Writing as Re-Vision," in *On Lies, Secrets, and Silence*; see especially p. 35.

58. *The Lost Tradition: Mothers and Daughters in Literature*, ed. Cathy N. Davidson and E. M. Broner (New York: Frederick Ungar Publishing, 1980).

59. Of course, the father figure is not necessarily presented as a heroic figure. Here, the father's heroism suggests the traditionally male concept of courage, bravery, aggression, etc. For examples of father figures who no longer fulfill the heroic deed, see the chapter "Faulkner's Sons of the Fathers," in MacKethan, *The Dream of Arcady*, pp. 153–180, especially pp. 154–155. Manning points out that the speech delivered by a friend at McKelva's funeral is a false tale about "romantic acts of heroism," as Laurel immediately recognizes (*With Ears Opening*, p. 171).

## CHAPTER 6

1. Patricia Tobin quotes this passage in her last chapter (*Time and the Novel*, p. 196). The quotation is from Roland Barthes, *The Pleasure of the Text*, trans. Richard Miller (New York: Hill and Wang, 1975), p. 47.

# Bibliography

## WORKS BY EUDORA WELTY

### Books

*The Bride of the Innisfallen and Other Stories*. New York: Harcourt Brace Jovanovich, 1955.

*The Collected Stories of Eudora Welty*. New York: Harcourt Brace Jovanovich, 1980.

*A Curtain of Green and Other Stories*. Garden City, N.Y.: Doubleday, Doran, 1941.

*Delta Wedding*. New York: Harcourt, Brace, 1946.

*The Golden Apples*. New York: Harcourt, Brace, 1949.

*Losing Battles*. New York: Random House, 1970.

*One Time, One Place*. New York: Random House, 1971.

*One Writer's Beginnings*. Cambridge, Mass.: Harvard University Press, 1984.

*The Optimist's Daughter*. New York: Random House, 1972.

*The Ponder Heart*. New York: Harcourt, Brace, 1954.

*The Robber Bridegroom*. Garden City, N.Y.: Doubleday, Doran, 1942.

*The Wide Net and Other Stories*. New York: Harcourt, Brace, 1943.

### Essays and Reviews

*The Eye of the Story: Selected Essays and Reviews*. New York: Random House, 1978.

"How I Write." *Virginia Quarterly* 31, No. 2 (Spring 1955), 240–251.

"Looking Back at the First Story." *Georgia Review* 33 (Winter 1979), 751–755.

## INTERVIEWS WITH WELTY

Buckley, William F., Jr. "The Southern Imagination: An Interview with Eudora Welty and Walker Percy." *Mississippi Quarterly* 26, No. 4 (Fall 1973), 493–516.

Bunting, Charles T. " 'The Interior World': An Interview with Eudora Welty." *Southern Review* 8 (October 1972), 711–735.

Devlin, Albert J. and Peggy Whitman Prenshaw. "A Conversation with Eudora Welty." *Mississippi Quarterly* 39, No. 4 (Fall 1986), 431–454.

Diamonstein, Barbaralee. "Eudora Welty." In *Open Secrets: Ninety-four Women in Touch with Our Times*. New York: Viking, 1972, pp. 442–445.

Gretlund, Jan Nordby. "An Interview with Eudora Welty." *Southern Humanities Review* 14 (Summer 1980), 193–208.

Jones, John Griffin. "Eudora Welty." *Mississippi Writers Talking*. Jackson, Miss.: University Press of Mississippi, 1982, pp. 3–35.

Kuehl, Linda. "The Art of Fiction XLVII: Eudora Welty." *Paris Review* 55 (Fall 1972), 72–97.

Prenshaw, Peggy Whitman, ed. *Conversations with Eudora Welty*. Jackson, Miss.: University Press of Mississippi, 1984.

van Noppen, Martha. "A Conversation with Eudora Welty." *The Southern Quarterly* 20 (Summer 1982), 7–23.

## WORKS ABOUT WELTY

### Bibliographies

McHaney, Pearl Amelia. "A Eudora Welty Checklist: 1973–1986." *Mississippi Quarterly* 39, No. 4 (Fall 1986). Special Eudora Welty issue, 651–697.

Polk, Noel. "A Eudora Welty Checklist." *Mississippi Quarterly* 26, No. 4 (Fall 1973). Special Eudora Welty issue, 663–693.

Swearingen, Bethany C. *Eudora Welty: A Critical Bibliography, 1936–1958*. Jackson, Miss.: University Press of Mississippi, 1984.

Thompson, Victor H. *Eudora Welty: A Reference Guide*. Boston: G. K. Hall, 1976.

### Books, Monographs, Essay Collections

Appel, Alfred. *A Season of Dreams: The Fiction of Eudora Welty*. Baton Rouge: Louisiana State University Press, 1965.

Bloom, Harold, ed. *Eudora Welty*. Modern Critical Views Series. New York: Chelsea, 1986.

Bryant, J. A., Jr. *Eudora Welty*. Pamphlets on American Writers. Minneapolis: University of Minnesota Press, 1968.

Desmond, John F., ed. *A Still Moment: Essays on the Art of Eudora Welty*. Metuchen, N.J. and London: The Scarecrow Press, 1978.

Devlin, Albert J. *Eudora Welty's Chronicle: A Story of Mississippi Life*. Jackson, Miss.: University Press of Mississippi, 1983.

Devlin, Albert J., ed. *Mississippi Quarterly* 39, No. 4 (Fall 1986). Special Eudora Welty issue.

Dollarhide, Louis, and Ann J. Abadie, eds. *Eudora Welty: A Form of Thanks*. Jackson, Miss.: University Press of Mississippi, 1979.

Engling, Beate. *Humoristische Elemente in den Kurzgeschichten und Romanen der Suedstaatenschriftstellerin Eudora Welty*. Frankfurt am Main, Bern, New York, and Paris: Peter Lang, 1988.

Evans, Elizabeth. *Eudora Welty*. New York: Frederick Ungar, 1981.

Graham, Kenneth, ed. *Delta*, No. 5 (November 1977). Eudora Welty issue.

Howard, Zelma Turner. *The Rhetoric of Eudora Welty's Short Stories*. Jackson, Miss.: University Press of Mississippi, 1973.

Isaacs, Neil D. *Eudora Welty*. Southern Writers Series. Austin: Steck-Vaughn Company, 1969.

Kreyling, Michael. *Eudora Welty's Achievement of Order*. Baton Rouge and London: Louisiana State University Press, 1980.

Manning, Carol S. *With Ears Opening Like Morning Glories: Eudora Welty and the Love of Storytelling*. Westport, Conn., and London: Greenwood Press, 1985.

Manz-Kunz, Marie-Antoinette. *Eudora Welty: Aspects of Reality in Her Short Fiction*. Swiss Studies in English. Bern: Francke Verlag, 1971.

Opitz, Karl. *Neoromantik als Gestalterin der Prosa Eudora Weltys*. Ph.D. diss., Free University of Berlin, 1959.

Prenshaw, Peggy Whitman, ed. *Eudora Welty: Critical Essays*. Jackson, Miss.: University Press of Mississippi, 1979.

Prenshaw, Peggy Whitman, ed. *Eudora Welty: Thirteen Essays*. Selected from *Eudora Welty: Critical Essays*. Jackson, Miss.: University Press of Mississippi, 1983.

Randisi, Jennifer Lynn. *A Tissue of Lies: Eudora Welty and the Southern Romance*. Washington, D.C., University Press of America, 1982.

Seele, Heide. *Eudora Weltys "The Optimist's Daughter": ein Roman der Ambiquitaet*. Ph.D. diss., University of Heidelberg, 1975.

Simpson, Lewis P., ed. *Mississippi Quarterly* 26, No. 4 (Fall 1973). Special Eudora Welty issue.

Vande Kieft, Ruth M. *Eudora Welty*. Twayne's United States Authors Series. New York: Twayne, 1962. rev. ed. Boston: Twayne, 1987.

Weiner, Rachel. "Reflections of the Artist in Eudora Welty's Fiction." Ph.D. diss., University of North Carolina, Chapel Hill, 1978.

Westling, Louise. *Sacred Groves and Ravaged Gardens: The Fiction of Eudora Welty, Carson McCullers, and Flannery O'Connor*. Athens, Ga.: The University of Georgia Press, 1985.

Westling, Louise. *Eudora Welty*. Basingstoke and London: Macmillan, 1989.

## Articles and Reviews

Arnold, Marilyn. "Images of Memory in Eudora Welty's *The Optimist's Daughter*." *Southern Literary Journal* 14 (Spring 1982), 28–38.

Boatwright, James. Review of *Losing Battles*. *New York Times Book Review* VII, 1 (April 12, 1970), pp. 32–34.

Boatwright, James. "Speech and Silence in *Losing Battles*." *Shenandoah* 25 (Spring 1974), 3–14.

Carson, Franklin. " 'The Song of Wandering Aengus': Allusions in Eudora Welty's *The Golden Apples*." *Notes on Mississippi Writers* 6 (Spring 1973), 14–18.

Carson, Franklin. "Recurring Metaphors: An Aspect of Unity in *The Golden Apples*." *Notes on Contemporary Literature* 5 (September 1975), 4–7.

Fritz-Piggot, Jill. "The Sword and The Song: Moments of Intensity in *The Golden Apples*." *Southern Literary Journal* 18, No. 2 (Spring 1986), 27–39.

Goudie, Andrea. "Eudora Welty's 'Circe': A Goddess Who Strove with Men." *Studies in Short Fiction* 13 (Fall 1976), 481–489.

Gossett, Louise Y. "Violence as Revelation: Eudora Welty," in Louise Y. Gossett, *Violence in Recent Southern Fiction*. Durham, N.C.: Duke University Press, 1965, pp. 98–117.

Hardy, John Edward. "*Delta Wedding* as Region and Symbol." *Sewanee Review* 60 (Summer 1952), 397–417.

Hardy, John Edward. "Eudora Welty's Negroes," in Seymour Gross and John Edward Hardy, eds., *Images of the Negro in American Literature*. Chicago: University of Chicago Press, 1966, pp. 221–232.

Isaacs, Neil D. "Four Notes on Eudora Welty." *Notes on Mississippi Writers* 2 (Fall 1969), 42–54.

Marrs, Suzanne. "The Making of *Losing Battles*: Plot Revision." *Southern Literary Journal* 18, No. 1 (Fall 1985), 40–49.

Messerli, Douglas. "The Problem of Time in Welty's *Delta Wedding*." *Studies in American Fiction* 5 (Fall 1977), 227–240.

Morris, Harry C. "Eudora Welty's Use of Mythology." *Shenandoah* 6 (Spring 1955), 34–40.

Oates, Joyce Carol. "Eudora's Web." *Atlantic Monthly* 225 (April 1970), 118–120, 122.

Pei, Lowry. "Dreaming the Other in *The Golden Apples*." *Modern Fiction Studies* 28, No. 3 (Fall 1982), 415–433.

Pitavy, Danièle. " 'Shower of Gold' ou les ambiguïtés de la narration." *Delta* 5 (November 1977), 63–81.

Pitavy-Souques, Danièle. "Watchers and Watching: Point of View in Eudora Welty's 'June Recital.' " Trans. Margaret Tomarchio. *Southern Review* 19 (Summer 1983), 483–509.

Pitavy-Souques, Danièle. "Le Sud: territoire des femmes?" *Revue Française D'Etudes Américaines* 10 (February 1985), 25–50.

Prenshaw, Peggy Whitman. "Cultural Patterns in Eudora Welty's *Delta Wedding* and 'The Demonstrators.' " *Notes on Mississippi Writers* 3 (Fall 1970 , 51–70.

Price, Reynolds. "The Onlooker, Smiling: An Early Reading of *The Optimist's Daughter*," in Reynolds Price, *Things Themselves: Essays & Scenes*. New York: Atheneum, 1972, pp. 114–138.

Pugh, Elaine Upton. "The Duality of Morgana: The Making of Virgie's Vision, the Vision of *The Golden Apples*." *Modern Fiction Studies* 28, No. 3 (Fall 1982), 435–451.

Rubin, Louis D., Jr. "Everything Brought Out into the Open: Eudora Welty's *Losing Battles*," in Louis Rubin, *William Elliott Shoots a Bear: Essays on the Southern Literary Imagination*. Baton Rouge: Louisiana State University Press, 1975, pp. 213–225.

Sprengnether, Madelon. "*Delta Wedding* and the Kore Complex." *Southern Quarterly* 25, No. 2 (Winter 1987), 120–130.

Stuckey, William J. "The Use of Marriage in Welty's *The Optimist's Daughter*." *Critique* 17, No. 2 (1975), 36–46.

Trilling, Diana. Review of *Delta Wedding*. *The Nation* (May 11, 1946), p. 578.

Tedford, Barbara Wilkie. "West Virginia Touches in Eudora Welty's Fiction." *Southern Literary Journal* 18, No. 2 (Spring 1986), 40–52.

Thornton, Naoko Fuwa. "Medusa-Perseus Symbolism in Eudora Welty's *The Optimist's Daughter*." *Southern Quarterly* 23, No. 4 (Summer 1985), 64–76.

Warren, Robert Penn. "The Love and the Separateness in Miss Welty." *Kenyon Review* 6 (Spring 1944), 246–259.

Yaeger, Patricia. "The Case of the Dangling Signifier: Phallic Imagery in Eudora Welty's 'Moon Lake.' " *Twentieth Century Literature* 28, No. 4 (Winter 1982), 431–452.

Yaeger, Patricia. " 'Because a Fire Was in My Head': Eudora Welty and the Dialogic Imagination." *PMLA* 99, No. 5 (Fall 1984), 955–973.

Young, Daniel Thomas. "Social Forms and Social Order: Eudora Welty's *The Optimist's Daughter*," in Daniel Thomas Young, *The Past in the Present: A Thematic Study of Modern Southern*

*Fiction*. Baton Rouge and London: Louisiana State University Press, 1981, pp. 87–115.

## OTHER SOURCES

Abel, Elizabeth, Marianne Hirsch, and Elizabeth Langland, eds. *The Voyage In: Fictions of Female Development*. Hanover, N.H. and London: University Press of New England, 1983.

Ardener, Edwin. "The 'Problem' Revisited," in *Perceiving Women*, ed. Shirley Ardener. New York: Halsted Press, 1975, pp. 19–27.

Cash, W. J. *The Mind of the South*. New York: Random House, 1941.

Chatman, Seymour. "The Structure of Narrative Transmission," in *Style and Structure in Literature*, ed. Roger Fowler. Ithaca, N.Y.: Cornell University Press, 1975, pp. 213–257.

Chodorow, Nancy. "Gender, Relation, and Difference in Psychoanalytic Perspective," in *The Future of Difference*, ed. Hester Eisenstein and Alice Jardine. New Brunswick, N.J.: Rutgers University Press, 1985, pp. 3–19.

Cohn, Dorrit. *Transparent Minds: Narrative Modes for Presenting Consciousness in Fiction*. Princeton, N.J.: Princeton University Press, 1978.

Davidson, Cathy, and E. M. Broner, eds. *The Lost Tradition: Mothers and Daughters in Literature*. New York: Frederick Ungar, 1980.

DuPlessis, Rachel Blau. *Writing beyond the Ending: Narrative Strategies of Twentieth Century Women Writers*. Bloomington, Ind.: Indiana University Press, 1985.

Edwards, Lee R. *Psyche as Hero: Female Heroism and Fictional Form*. Middletown, Conn.: Wesleyan University Press, 1984.

Flax, Jane. "Mother-Daughter Relationships: Psychodynamics, Politics, and Philosophy," in *The Future of Difference*, ed. Hester Eisenstein and Alice Jardine. New Brunswick, N.J.: Rutgers University Press, 1985.

Gardiner, Judith Kegan. "On Female Identity and Writing by Women," in *Writing and Sexual Difference*, ed. Elizabeth Abel. Chicago: University of Chicago Press, 1982, pp. 177–191.

Gray, Richard. *The Literature of Memory: Modern Writers of the American South*. London: Edward Arnold, 1977.

Hoffman, Frederick. *The Art of Southern Fiction*. Carbondale, Ill., and Edwardsville, Ill.: Southern Illinois University Press, 1967.

Holman, Hugh C. *Three Modes of Modern Fiction: Ellen Glasgow, William Faulkner, Thomas Wolfe*. Athens, Ga.: University of Georgia Press, 1966.

Holman, Hugh C. *The Immoderate Past: The Southern Writer and History*. Athens, Ga.: University of Georgia Press, 1977.

Jones, Anne Goodwyn. *Tomorrow Is Another Day: The Woman Writer in the South, 1859–1936*. Baton Rouge and London: Louisiana State University Press, 1981.

Kolodny, Annette. "Dancing through the Minefield: Some Observations on the Theory, Practice and Politics of a Feminist Literary Criticism." *Feminist Studies* 6, No. 1 (Spring 1979), 1–25.

Kristeva, Julia. "Women's Time." Trans. Alice Jardine and Harry Blake. *Signs* 1 (Fall 1981), 5–35.

Lanser, Susan Sniader. *The Narrative Act: Point of View in Prose Fiction*. Princeton, N.J.: Princeton University Press, 1981.

McConnell-Ginet, Sally, Ruth Borker, and Nelly Furman, eds. *Women and Language in Literature and Society*. Praeger Special Studies. New York: Praeger Publishers, 1980.

MacKethan, Lucinda Hardwick. *The Dream of Arcady: Place and Time in Southern Literature*. Baton Rouge and London: Louisiana State University Press, 1980.

Marks, Elaine, and Isabelle de Courtivron, eds. *New French Feminisms*. New York: Schocken Books, 1981.

Moers, Ellen. *Literary Women*. London: The Women's Press, 1978.

Pearson, Carol, and Katherine Pope. *The Female Hero in American and British Literature*. New York and London: R. R. Bowker, 1981.

Pratt, Annis. *Archetypal Patterns in Women's Fiction*. Bloomington, Ind.: Indiana University Press, 1981.

Rich, Adrienne. *Of Woman Born: Motherhood as Experience and Institution*. New York: W. W. Norton, 1976.

Rich, Adrienne, "When We Dead Awaken: Writing as Re-Vision," in Adrienne Rich, *On Lies, Secrets, and Silence: Se-*

*lected Prose 1966–1978*. New York: W. W. Norton, 1979, pp. 33–49.

Rubin, Louis D., Jr. *Writers of the Modern South: The Faraway Country*. Seattle and London: University of Washington Press, 1963.

Rubin, Louis D., Jr. *The American South: Portrait of a Culture*. Baton Rouge and London: Louisiana State University Press, 1980.

Scholes, Robert. *Structuralism in Literature: An Introduction*. New Haven, Conn., and London: Yale University Press, 1974.

Showalter, Elaine. *A Literature of Their Own: British Novelists from Brontë to Lessing*. Princeton, N.J.: Princeton University Press, 1977.

Showalter, Elaine. "Feminist Criticism in the Wilderness," in *Writing and Sexual Difference*, ed. Elizabeth Abel. Chicago: University of Chicago Press, 1982, pp. 9–35.

Spacks, Patricia Meyer. *The Female Imagination*. New York: Alfred A. Knopf, 1975.

Tobin, Patricia Drechsel. *Time and the Novel: The Genealogical Imperative*. Princeton, N.J.: Princeton University Press, 1978.

Woolf, Virginia. *Women and Writing*. London: The Women's Press, 1979.

# Index

## ABOUT THE AUTHOR

FRANZISKA GYGAX is a Research Fellow of the Swiss Foundation for the Sciences and Humanities in Switzerland and a Visiting Fellow at the English Department at Princeton University. Her publications include "Gertrude Stein and the Deconstruction of the Family": *The Making of Americans* in *Women in Search of a Literary Space*, ed. Katrina Bachinger, Gudrun Grabher, and Maureen Lange-Devine, (forthcoming).